English as a Language of Teaching and Learning for Community Secondary Schools in Tanzania

English as a Language of Teaching and Learning for Community Secondary Schools in Tanzania

A Critical Analysis

ELIA SHABANI MLIGO
and
MIKAEL KAOMBEKA MWASHILINDI

Foreword by Emmanuel Y. Mbogo
Preface by Joshua S. Madumulla

RESOURCE *Publications* • Eugene, Oregon

ENGLISH AS A LANGUAGE OF TEACHING AND LEARNING FOR COMMUNITY SECONDARY SCHOOLS IN TANZANIA
A Critical Analysis

Copyright © 2017 Elia Shabani Mligo and Mikael Kaombeka Mwashilindi. All rights reserved. Except for brief quotations in critical publications or reviews, no part of this book may be reproduced in any manner without prior written permission from the publisher. Write: Permissions, Wipf and Stock Publishers, 199 W. 8th Ave., Suite 3, Eugene, OR 97401.

Resource Publications
An Imprint of Wipf and Stock Publishers
199 W. 8th Ave., Suite 3
Eugene, OR 97401

www.wipfandstock.com

PAPERBACK ISBN: 978-1-5326-1875-8
HARDCOVER ISBN: 978-1-4982-4455-8
EBOOK ISBN: 978-1-4982-4454-1

Manufactured in the U.S.A.   JULY 31, 2017

With great love, this book is dedicated to Mligo's late mother Tuladzuma Ngella and Mwashilindi's late mother Mailen Yohan Simbeye for their genuine parental care.

"It is now clearly time for us to think seriously about this question: what is the education system in Tanzania intended to do—what is its purpose? Having decided that, we have to look at the tasks it has to do. In the light of that examination we can consider whether, in our present circumstances, further modifications are required or whether we need a change in the whole approach."
—Nyerere, Education for Self-Reliance, 1967.

"As a matter of efficiency and efficacy, only the language which teachers and students understand can effectively function as the language of instruction. Only when teachers and students understand the language of instruction are they able to discuss, debate, ask and answer questions, ask for clarification and therefore construct and generate knowledge. These are activities that are a pre-requisite to learning and whose level determines the quality of education. Thus, the language of instruction is an important factor in determining the quality of education."
—Qorro, "Does Language of Instruction affect Quality?" 3.

"*Kulingana na wataalamu wa masuala ya saikolojia ya elimu lugha inayofaa kutumika kutolea maarifa kwa wananchi ni ile ambayo wananchi husika wanaifahamu na wanaielewa vyema.*" [According to scholars of psychology of education, the language suitable to be used in teaching knowledge to people in a certain country is that which people of that country know and understand it well.]
—Gawasike, "Lugha ya Kiswahili," 75.

Contents

List of Tables and Charts | *x*
Foreword by Emmanuel Y. Mbogo | *xi*
Preface by Joshua S. Madumulla | *xiii*
Acknowledgments | *xxi*
Abbreviations | *xxiii*

Chapter 1: Introduction | 1

    Background of the Problem and Experiences
    Brief History of Education in Tanzania
    Education and Kiswahili Language
    Community Secondary Schools in Tanzania
    Problem and Objectives
    Significance of the Book

Chapter 2: Looking Back: Review of Related Literatures | 31

    Introduction
    English as a Medium for Teaching and Learning
    English Language at a Global Level
    English Language in Africa
    English Language in Tanzania
    Teaching and Learning Using Other Languages
    The Emerging Gap of Knowledge
    Conclusion

Contents

Chapter 3: Laying Out the Way: Hypothesis and Methodology | 54

    Introduction
    Hypothesis and Design
    Area of Study and Sources of Data
        Primary Sources
        Secondary Sources
    Population and Sample
    Instruments for Data Collection
    Data Analysis and Presentation
    Conclusion

Chapter 4: Hearing from Educational Stakeholders: Data Presentation and Discussion | 66

    Introduction
    Mbeya District Council as an Area of Research
        Administration and Land Area
        Transport and Communication
        Water and Energy Supply
        Socio-economic and Agricultural Information
        Industries, Forests, and People's Population
        Educational Information
    Teachers' and Students' General Responses
    Performance in Form Four Summative Examinations
    The Study and Use of English: Responses from Close-Ended Questionnaires
        English Language and Academic Performance
        English Language and Ages of Respondents
        English Language and Availability of Books
        English Language and Teachers' Availability
        English Language and Teachers' Teaching Experiences
        English Language Proficiency and Students' Failure in Examinations
        Teachers' Fluency in English Language

    Knowledge of English Language and Students' Academic Performance
        Students' Ability to Read English Language
        Students' Ability to Speak English Language
        Students' Ability to Listen and Understand English Language
        Students' Ability to Write English
    Students' Inability to Use English as Their Language of Learning
    Students' Poor Performance in Form Four Examinations
    Towards improving the Use of English as Language of Teaching and Learning

Chapter 5: Conclusion | 122

References | 135
Name Index | 145
Subject Index | 149

List of Tables and Charts

A Sketch of Education System in Tanzania Mainland | 18

Table 1   District Area, Number of Divisions, Wards, Villages and Hamlets | 70

Table 2   Distribution of Population in Each Division | 73

Table 3   Overall Students' Responses Obtained from the Field | 75–79

Table 4   Overall Teachers' Responses Obtained from the Field | 81–82

Table 5   Overall Performance of Students in the Sampled Secondary Schools | 84

Table 6   Poor Knowledge of English as a Contributing Factor to Poor Performance | 86

Table 7   Ages of Respondents | 88

Table 9   Availability of Books | 89

Table 9   Teachers Availability | 91

Table 10   Teachers' Experience | 93

Table 11   English Proficiency and Students' Failure | 94

Table 12   Teachers Fluency in English | 98

Table 13   Ability to Read English | 101

Table 14   Ability to Speak English | 103

Table 15   Ability to listen and Understand English | 104

Table 16   Ability to Write English | 106

Foreword

To date extensive research has been done by many scholars on whether English or Kiswahili should be used as a medium of instruction for both lower and higher learning institution in Tanzania. There are books and conference papers which have been written on the subject. Our libraries have substantial stock of theses and dissertations whose theme revolves around this same debate. However, in: *English as a Language of Teaching and Learning for Community Secondary Schools in Tanzania*, Elia Shabani Mligo and Mikael Kaombeka Mwashilindi's research focuses mainly on the difficulties for English, a foreign language, to fit as a medium of instruction in the Tanzanian context. The question asked is: how and when will English proficiency be achieved by students at both primary and secondary school levels? The study which focuses on selected Community Secondary schools in Mbeya District Council provides strong practical recommendations in the final concluding chapter.

However, in the Tanzanian context, there is no way one can discuss and research on English as a medium of instruction without relating it to both Kiswahili and vernacular languages spoken by millions of people across the country. It should be noted that, it is a half a century since Tanzania mainland attained her independence in 1961, and yet the Ministry of Education and the government at large, have not made a bold and firm decision on the use of either English or Kiswahili as a medium of instruction from primary all the way to institutions of higher learning.

Mligo and Mwashilindi have, in this extensive research, underlined the fact that in government primary schools, which are the majority, all subjects are taught in Kiswahili while English is hardly given emphasis.

Foreword

Students hardly get the opportunity to practice written and spoken English. To make matters worse, most English teachers for primary schools are very poor in both written and spoken English, and therefore code-switching becomes the norm; and under such circumstances, by the time a student finishes primary education he/she is completely incapable of using English fluently.

As the two authors emphasize, when these students join secondary schools, they are subjected to a sudden transition whereby all subjects are taught in English; acquiring knowledge and comprehension of facts becomes a cumbersome and boring process. Students who proved to be intelligent in primary schools tend to perform poorly. Given this scenario, at the end of form four Students fail their exams not because they are stupid, but because of poor English background.

On the other hand, as exemplified by the two authors in this study, English is equally important and relevant not only for acquiring knowledge through millions of publications and materials written in English; but also for general communication in areas such as socioeconomic development, science, technology and culture. And this can be achieved not by replacing Kiswahili with English, but first a need to train enough skilled and competent English teachers who will teach it as a subject and invest heavily in the production of teaching materials and make them available to students and teachers all over the country.

On the other extreme, I would argue, any attempt to make English language a medium of instruction at primary school level in order to have one language used for teaching and learning from lower levels to higher ones will not be the best option. Authors of this book have provided sufficient reasons and evidence for this argument. Finally, I want to sincerely thank the two authors for having given me this honor of writing a foreword to this very important publication.

Professor Emmanuel Y. Mbogo (PhD)
The Open University of Tanzania
Dar es Salaam Tanzania
March 2017

Preface

"I hate Mathematics because I do not understand it. The teacher uses English in teaching and wants us to ask questions in English while we are not conversant with that language because of our poor foundation of English language when we were in Primary school...."

(Extracted from this book, page 104)

The foregoing statement is a confession by a student in a community secondary school in Tanzania. By implication and assumption, the statement is both an inclusive and collective voice of students facing the same predicament. The predicament of using English, a foreign language, which is unfortunately, not well understood by most students and even by some teachers. It is this predicament which is being addressed in this book under the title: *English as a Language of Teaching and Learning for Community Secondary Schools in Tanzania*. It is, indeed, a predicament that has attracted the attention of a number of scholars who have discussed it under the theme of what medium of instruction should be for quality education, quality communication, and even quality development. Again, by implication and assumption, the same statement could be uttered by the same category of students indicating hatred against any other subject taught in English (or any other medium of instruction in which they are not well-versed).

With that prologue, let us now comprehend what is meant by a community secondary school. In Tanzania there are three categories of

Preface

education authorities, namely, government, local (native) and private. The education institutions under the government authority make the majority. Those under private authority are two-pronged: there are institutions that are owned by individual persons and there are those owned by organizations, where the religious ones take the lead. The Native (local) authority has been running the education institutions which are Ward-based. In the latest years each Ward has been encouraged to have a secondary school with science laboratories. The schools under the Native Authority are the ones referred to as community schools, because they are cared for by the communities. The said schools have happened to face a number of challenges, owing to monetary, as well as monitory constraints. However, currently the community schools are not that much apparently noticed, because they appear to be covered behind the curtain of the government authority. The government and private institutions have been performing better, because of better workforce and facilities.

Stephen M. Neke argues that the "use of English as a medium of instruction in post-primary education in Tanzania raises issues of language education policy, of relations between English, education, and science, and of access to opportunities and economic dependency. It also underlies questions of power relations and of resource distribution."[1] It is further argued that "language education policy decisions are socio-economic, since they entail a reversal of power relations and *may lead to certain groups in the community, whose language is not selected, finding themselves at the fringes of the socio-economic and political spectrum.*"[2] It is Neke's point of view that a medium of instruction should be carefully sorted out in order that it should not be divisive in serving a given community. The authors of this book are also in consensus with Neke when they state that the main endeavour of any meaningful educational policy is to ensure the provision of quality education at all levels of education.[3]

Casmir M. Rubagumya has widely discussed the issue of a medium of instruction in Tanzania, where he feels there is a conflict of aspirations and achievements, on the one hand, while on the other hand, there are some problems with the language planning in the education system of Tanzania that need redressing.[4] Earlier on, Phillipson outlined what he referred to as

1. Neke, "The Medium of Instruction," 73.
2. Neke, "The Medium of Instruction," 73(emphasis of quoted materials is ours).
3. Ibid.
4. Rubagumya, "English-medium Instruction," 107.

Preface

tenets which guided the practice of a Language of Instruction (LoI) in Anglophone Africa, that: (i) English is best taught as a monolingual language; (ii) "the earlier English is taught to children, the better the results"; (iii) "if other languages are used much, then the standards of English will drop"; (iv) "the more English is taught, the better the results," and (v) the native speaker of a particular language can teach that language better.[5] Much as these tenets are directed only to English language teaching, they actually apply to the teaching of any language. Thus, in the place of 'English' it could be substituted by 'a language'.

There are those scholars who prefer the UNESCO approach in the discussion of what they feel an effective medium of instruction should be. To them, it is that which considers that providing education in a child's mother tongue is a central issue. To most of Tanzanians (over 95%) a foreign language, including English, is a third language, preceded by Kiswahili and their local (vernacular) languages. Herman M. Batibo, Martha Qorro and F.E.M.K. Senkoro view Kiswahili as a local national language used by about 95% of the entire population, while English is spoken fluently and used by only about 5% of the population. If we go for actual figures, in 2010 Kiswahili was the medium of instruction in 15,816 public primary schools nationwide, while English was the medium of instruction in 539 of the 551 registered private primary schools.[6] Therefore, the proponents of Kiswahili argue that it is Kiswahili, and not English, that is popular among most Tanzanians in performing their official and daily chores. Further to their mind, Tanzania made several efforts, especially in the 1980s and 1990s to have Kiswahili as LoI (refer to Makweta's Commission that recommended Kiswahili to be the LoI at all levels of education), but never took off, because the British government convinced the government of Tanzania that they would assist in strengthening English language by funding the implementation of the English Language Support Project (ELSP). However, the proponents of Kiswahili as LoI have continually been of the opinion that Kiswahili be the LoI at all levels of education, while strengthening English as a subject.[7]

There is also a sign of indifference which appears to be the result of self-denigration. It can be traced through a "study conducted by Rubagumya

---

5. Phillipson, *Linguistic Imperialism*, 185–212.

6. Cf. Wikipedia, "Education in Tanzania."

7. Batibo, "The Growth of Kiswahili as Language of Education," Qorro, "Language of Instruction," and Senkoro, "Language of Instruction."

Preface

in 1991 cited in Roy-Campbell (1995) on the attitude of some Tanzanians towards English as LoI which found that, while 65% of the respondents were more comfortable with Kiswahili, 53% felt that *education standards would deteriorate* if Kiswahili became the medium of instruction."[8] It is the feeling of Rubagumya, and correctly so, that "at present, much of the public debate concerning the choice between English or Kiswahili as the LoI in Tanzanian education fails to take account of the distinction between *using a language for learning* and *learning a language*."[9] A succinct addition is made by Qorro who points out that "quality education is that which is capable of bringing about change in learners: from less knowledge to more knowledge; less confident to more confident; dependent to independence; job seekers to job creators. . . . "[10] This change can be obtained through "making a concerted effort to have the kind of education which encourages learners to take an active part in the learning process. . . . "[11]

The authors of this book carried out their study guided by their hypothesis that poor performance in Form IV summative examinations in community secondary schools was caused by the low proficiency of English in students, as well as in their teachers. The study examined the relationship between the use of English which is poorly understood by both teachers and students, on the one hand, and the quality of education obtained by the use of this foreign language in teaching and learning in these community secondary schools.

The authors noted with emphasis the dearth of and quest for a LoI in Tanzania. If the LoI must be English, their research findings point to salient challenges in a form of weaknesses that must be remedied. A few of them include: Some stakeholder's ignorance of educational policy on LoI; using teachers who are not competent in English language; using teachers who never went through teacher training programs for teaching methods; truancy; economically incapacitated families; code-switching; taking failures at secondary and high schools to join the teaching profession as a damping area; rote learning methods; lack of motivation; and lack of practice, among others. In the bid to combat the weaknesses and strive for quality education through a foreign, not well-comprehended LOI, the authors came up with

---

8. Essays, UK. "Language of Instruction."
9. Rubagumya, "Language Values."
10. Qorro, "Does Language of Instruction affect Quality?" 9.
11. Ibid.

PREFACE

the following recommendations, whose enumeration hereunder does not suggest a priority ordering:

i. There is a need to establish debate clubs in community secondary schools in order to build language fluency and self-confidence;

ii. Need to avoid code-switching and code-mixing in and outside the classroom, again, for the purpose of building language fluency;

iii. The government through education policy to make one language (Kiswahili or English) a LoI in all education levels, where the mother tongue could be given a priority and the other language remain as a subject, but taught well;

iv. If the LoI is a foreign language (in this case, English), the use of Kiswahili and vernacular languages should be discouraged or limited;

v. Teachers and parents should motivate students to perform well in language studies/learning;

vi. Teachers should give to students an assortment of meaningful assignments in the form of writing and reading;

vii. The government should recruit competent language teachers who will be role models to their students;

viii. The government should not enrol failure students to join the teaching profession. It has been found through various researches that "academically weak students have been flooding teacher education" programs in education institutions in Tanzania and "enrolling such under-qualified candidates has had far-reaching" implications in the teaching and learning process;[12]

ix. The government should ensure that all Lecturers or teachers in education related academic units must be products of the teacher training curriculum. Unless one went through the teacher training program, s/he should not be offered a place to teach in the School/Faculty or Department at a University;

x. Tutorial Assistants (TAs) should not be given courses to teach at degree level, because they are academics who hold first degrees and are supposed to supervise seminars under the tutelage of senior staff;

12. Kitta & Fussy, "Bottlenecks in Preparation of Quality Teachers," 33.

PREFACE

xi. The salaries and remuneration of teachers should be improved for the purpose of attracting students to the teaching profession, as well as for retention;

xii. The Ministry of Education, Science and Technology should ensure that there are enough and qualified language teachers in community secondary schools;

xiii. The mass-media should be carefully used to promoting education in the country through enhancement of effective use of language. Ineffective use of media tarnishes people's names and dignities, or causes misunderstandings and even wars and violence;[13]

xiv. Strongly recognize the position of the parents by encouraging them to support their children by:
- affording materials for learning,
- teaching them at home,
- helping them to complete their homework,
- being role models to them,
- giving them parental love through balanced diet, clothing, mentoring and entertainment, and
- visiting their schools;

xv. There should be enough language periods in the school timetable;

xvi. For the private sector dealing with education, they should make it easily and reasonably affordable by arranging costs that are not too high; and

xvii. There is a need for further research on this controversial subject on LOI nationally, regionally, and worldwide.

This book is an important contribution to the hot discussion about the *means* of attaining quality education, which must be no other thing but a language that is delivered well. No nation can compete successfully in a globalized world drilled with highly sophisticated and fast changing scientific and technological advancement without a perfected means of communication. No wonder, as the authors have just argued, the book sets up controversial-cum-rhetorical questions: Is English an appropriate language of instruction to pre-primary and primary schools as is now used by private English Medium pre-primary and primary schools under the

13. Mugyenyi, *Aspects of Sociology*, 17–19.

State's prepared curriculums and syllabuses? Is English an appropriate language of instruction to Ordinary and Advanced Level secondary schools in Tanzania, with the majority students from State owned primary schools using Kiswahili as LoI? Is English an appropriate language of instruction to higher-learning Colleges, and Universities of Tanzania, especially at undergraduate level? Does the use of English language as a language of teaching and learning in Tanzanian Colleges and Universities properly prepare experts who are well-equipped to serve in a Tanzanian society, whose main language of communication is Kiswahili? Or, does it prepare graduates with a mentality of working in English-speaking countries and unfit to work in the Tanzanian context? These questions are foods for thought to education policy-makers and stakeholders.

Professor Joshua S. Madumulla (PhD)
University of Iringa
Iringa, Tanzania
March 2017

Acknowledgments

We wish to take this opportunity to acknowledge the following for their contributions towards the accomplishment of this book. First, our vote of thanks goes to the Almighty God, who kept us safe and healthy throughout the research and report writing process. Second, we appreciate the generosity of the Mbeya Regional Administrative Secretary, Mbeya District Council, for the permission to do research in Mbeya District Council. Third, we humbly recognize the warm welcome we received from the Heads of Imezu, Iwalanje, Nsongwi Juu and Usongwe Secondary Schools, and for the permission to do research in their schools. Fourth, we honor the contribution of all teachers and students who were involved in this exercise. Their contributions were tremendously important for the completion of this book. Fifth, Prof. Emmanuel Y. Mbogo (from the Open University of Tanzania) and Prof. Joshua S. Madumulla (from the University of Iringa, Tanzania) for reading, commenting, and writing the Foreword and Preface respectively. Sixth, the research for this book was done under the auspices of Tumaini University Makumira–Mbeya Teaching Centre, Mbeya Tanzania. We greatly appreciate for their support through the Research and Consultancy Section. Seventh, we are indebted to the editors and typesetters at Wipf and Stock Publishers, Eugene Oregon, for their excellent work. This book could not be in the form it has now without them. Finally, the two secretaries of Mbeya Teaching Centre, Neema Alex Kapalila and Agnes Syoge Kagelelo, for typing this book manuscript in the computer and making the corrections of subsequent drafts. However, none of the above-mentioned contributors is responsible for any mistake within this book. The responsibility remains ours. Moreover, all the literal translations from

ACKNOWLEDGMENTS

Kiswahili to English in this book are ours, unless stated otherwise. May the Almighty God grant abundant mercy upon all people who contributed in one way or another towards the realization of this book!

Abbreviations

ACSE	Advanced Certificate of Secondary Education
BAKITA	Baraza la Kiswahili la Tanzania
B.A.Ed.	Bachelor of Arts with Education
BEST	Basic Educational Statistics in Tanzania
B.Sc.Ed.	Bachelor of Science with Education
CS	Code Switching
CSEE	Certificate of Secondary Education Examination
DEO	District Education Officer
DC	District Council
ELTSP	English Language Teaching Support Project
ESR	Education for Self-Reliance
FGD	Focus Group Discussion
GPA	Grade Point Average
LoI	Language of Instruction
MoEVT	Ministry of Education and Vocational Training
NACTE	National Council for Technical Education
NECTA	National Examinations Council of Tanzania
PGDE	Post-Graduate Diploma in Education

ABBREVIATIONS

SPSS	Statistical Package for Social Sciences
TA	Tutorial Assistant
TANU	Tanganyika African National Union
TAZARA	Tanzania Zambia Railways
TCU	Tanzania Commission for Universities
UPE	Universal Primary Education
URT	United Republic of Tanzania
UNESCO	United Nations Educational, Scientific and Cultural Organization
VETA	Vocational Education and Training Authority
WEC	Ward Education Coordinator

Chapter 1

Introduction

"Language of instruction is a vehicle through which education is delivered. The role of language of instruction can be likened to that of pipes in carrying water from one destination to another or that of copper wires in transmitting electricity from one station to another. Just as a pipe is an important medium in carrying water, and a copper wire an important medium for transmitting electricity, the language of instruction is an indispensable medium for carrying, or transmitting education from teachers to learners and among learners."

—Qorro, "Does Language of Instruction affect Quality?" 3

BACKGROUND OF THE PROBLEM AND EXPERIENCES

English is one of the worldwide spoken languages, probably the greatest spoken language of all.[1] Since it boasts a worldwide use, it has been one of the languages used for academic arenas as a language of instruction in

---

1. The concept of language means many things to many people depending on people and context. However, in this book we adopt Mchumbo's understanding which states: "Language resides in the patterns that the sounds or the markings [linguistic signs and symbols] on paper or variants thereof represent. Those sounds or markings constitute the mediums for linguistic representation. They are different, and they appeal to different cognitive skills for production, perception and processing." (Mchumbo, "Language, Learning and Education," 22) This understanding will enable us to discuss language as a medium of instruction in the four major skills: reading, writing, speaking, and understanding.

various educational levels worldwide.[2] This book assesses the way in which English is used as a teaching and learning medium in Community Secondary Schools in Tanzania. It investigates the effectiveness and shortcomings of using this language and thereby provides the possible recommendations.

The idea of conducting a study about the language of instruction in Tanzania originates from four major factors. The first factor relates to experiences we have had with Community Secondary Schools and in our own studies and interactions with people. Community Secondary Schools were schools with children who passed standard seven examinations, most of them being taught English with teachers who were themselves incapable of the language. Most students in those schools were not even able to make a single grammatically correct sentence. We outline the experiences from community secondary schools and from our own studies in the following paragraphs.

In the year 1992–1993 Mligo taught Biology and Chemistry at Makoga Secondary school in Njombe Tanzania, which was then a community secondary school. It was obvious from that school that most students were unable to perform well in classes. In 1993–1994 Mligo moved to Wanging'ombe Secondary School, also a community secondary school in Njombe District. The performance of students at this school was also poor. In both schools, Makoga and Wanging'ombe, students mostly showed dependence on the teachers in almost whatever they were to learn. Their participation in discussions during classes were minimal; and during their group discussions, most students used Kiswahili mixing it with English in order to grasp what they learned in class. Moreover, most of them were not willing to read text books in the library regarding what they learned in class. The questions that come out of this experience were the following: What was wrong with those Community Secondary Schools? Why their students were unable to fully grasp what was being taught in class when using English as a teaching medium? Why were they mostly reluctant to read textbooks? In fact, students in these schools learned English while at primary schools. They were supposed to use that language when in secondary school as a study medium. In most cases, this was not the case!

In 1995 Mligo joined University education at Makumira University College in Arusha Tanzania. When at Makumira University College, he and the other students of his class had to conduct research and write scientific research papers as partial fulfillments for their undergraduate studies. It

---

2. Wierzbicka, *English: Meaning and Culture*, 3.

was a difficult task to most of them to understand what it meant by research, how they should conduct it, and how they should report it in a scientific way. This difficulty was mainly caused by the language used—English language. This language was not their language. It was just the language of teaching and learning, the language they were hardly acquainted well during their secondary school studies. Therefore, research in its real sense, was a vocabulary which they did not hear before they went to university.

Moreover, the most difficult aspect to them was the switching of languages—from the language which was used to teach the research course in class to the language used to conduct research during fieldwork. They were taught research in English, and were supposed to prepare research tools and conduct research in Kiswahili during the data collection process at the field where Kiswahili was used predominantly. The challenge came when data were collected, and were to be transcribed into English, the language into which research reports were to be written. Since they were not fluent in English language, to change the collected data into English was a difficult task for them. In most cases, this change of languages caused improper presentation of the collected data as were collected from Kiswahili speaking research participants. Following this experience, Mligo started to sense that if the Tanzanian researcher understood research in the researcher's native language (Kiswahili), with the vocabulary which the researcher was both taught and used it in the fieldwork, and had been hearing since childhood, that researcher would be able to conduct it more properly.

Another issue of Mligo's experience in regard to English language concerns the ability of most Tanzanians to use this language in higher education. In 2005 Mligo joined Masters degree studies at the University of Oslo in Norway. At the University of Oslo, Mligo met three other Africans and several Europeans in his class. They were only four African students in that class. The other Africans were from Kenya, Zimbabwe and Ghana. In the communications that were done in class or somewhere else Mligo, a Tanzanian, was found incompetent in expressing himself fluently as compared to his other fellow Africans. However, this did not mean that he did not understand the taught subject matter if he were to study and express it in Kiswahili, the language he was more conversant. English seemed to be a bottleneck to him towards discussing issues freely, both in academic and normal communications. Mligo had to keep silent most of his time!

In the beginning of his studies at the University of Oslo, Mligo felt so inferior and thought he was the only Tanzanian student to be incompetent in English language. As his class started interactions with students from other faculties at the University, Mligo met with some other Tanzanians. It was clear that Tanzanian students from those faculties had a similar English language problem as his. This collective problem to most Tanzanians whom Mligo had academic interactions with them from other faculties at the University indicated that English was foreign to Tanzanians. Moreover, it was vivid that these Tanzanians spoke Kiswahili fluently among themselves in normal extra-academic affairs within the academic and non-academic campuses.

However, Mligo's observation during the time of stay in Norway for studies indicated that most of the countries in Europe used their native languages to teach students from lower levels of education to University level, except for some few programs designed for international students. For example, most, if not all, universities in Scandinavian countries, Germany, France, etc., used their native languages which students understood well and had been using them since childhood. For these countries, English was taught as a subject, not as a medium for teaching other subjects. This observation made Mligo raise some questions: Why do these countries emphasize on their own native languages for teaching and learning despite the prominent existing international languages? Why did they not use English for them to be international?

Mligo's other experience was from a Private Secondary School owned by the church. In 2004–2005, just after completing studies in Norway, Mligo was appointed to teach Advanced Level students (form VI) at this Private Secondary school located in Njombe District Tanzania. He used English language in teaching his course as the curriculum required him to do despite his language weakness. He strictly used English from beginning to end when teaching in class without code switching or code mixing between English with another language. Though there was a little students' participation in class discussions and poor performances to formative examinations, he did not dare to leave any chance for language mixing or switching. The English language was maintained during classes despite the vivid hardships facing students to master the taught content.

The consequence of this strict use of English was noted at the end of the planned subject, and after the summative examination was provided to students. Normally form six students at that particular school had class farewell parties. Students celebrated the two-year time they spent at the school and said words of goodbye to each other as each one departed home.

Introduction

Mligo was preferentially selected to participate in the farewell party of this class. A cake was prepared as a gift to congratulate him for his teaching strategy. When Mligo asked them as to why they considered selecting him alone over other teachers who taught the class, one student stood up and said to him: "You deserve this invitation and a small gift we have just prepared. This is because of the strict use of English language throughout your teaching in class. We have never witnessed any other teacher using English language throughout the time when teaching in class without switching to or mixing it with Kiswahili since we arrived in this school. You are the only one!" What did the student's words mean? What did their gift mean? Did it mean that students enjoyed being taught in English? The student's words and their gift had several meanings that could be constructed from them. However, to Mligo, this event mostly underlined the problem with the English language to both teachers and students, not only to that secondary school, but also to most other secondary schools within the country because the secondary school which Mligo taught incorporated students from almost all over the country.

The second factor is associated with the authors' experiences with the rural areas where there were very few teachers, particularly English teachers, no tuitions and English short courses, poor economic conditions of parents, and low education levels of parents making them have difficulties to help their children. The migration of people from rural to urban areas was no objection in Tanzania as it was in most other places of the world. Teachers with good qualifications preferred to stay in urban places where there were good allocations of social services for their lives. Since community secondary schools were mostly owned by private institutions, teachers were not allocated by the government to work there. They were employed by the school owners. This made most schools in rural areas lack competent teachers because of teachers' choices to work in urban places.

The third factor based on peoples' understanding of the importance of Education. Education is a fundamental human right as well as a catalyst for economic and social development. Education is valued because of its contribution to the national development. It is a useful human resource that helps to stimulate productivity and eliminate hunger, poverty, disease and ignorance. In fact this understanding is what was supposed to be shared in community secondary schools and the community surrounding these schools. This understanding greatly lacked in such schools and even to most teachers and students.

The last, but not least, factor was about students' poor performance in community secondary schools. In fact, every year we witnessed a mass failure of students in these schools as compared to students from Government and other Private secondary schools (e.g., religious owned secondary schools). This mass failure of students in these schools stimulated us towards knowing the cause of it; hence, this research.

In summary this sub-section has discussed the origin of the idea for conducting a study in regard to language use in Tanzania. We have discussed four major factors which stimulated us to deal with this topic and, therefore, the title of this book. We have discussed the factors at length for other scholars and readers of this book to clearly understand why it was important for us to do a study on this important issue.

BRIEF HISTORY OF EDUCATION IN TANZANIA

This sub-section briefly discusses the history of education in the African Continent, and Tanzania in particular. The sub-section explains how knowledge and skills were transmitted from one generation to another before the coming of Arabs and Europeans in the continent and the role of language of instruction in that context. The discussion is based on non-formal (out of school) education which was maintained by most Africans before the coming of Europeans and formal education which they brought to Africa. This discussion sets a stage for the next two sub-sections which will deal with the Kiswahili language and history of community secondary schools in Tanzania as part of formal education.

Long before the coming of Arabs and Europeans to Africa, the African people had developed their own systems of informal education for each ethnic group conducted through the tribal language of instruction. There was no problem concerning the language of instruction before the coming of colonialism where education was informal. The problem emerged after the introduction of formal education in the 1800s.[3] Informal education "is a form of education an individual derives from the environment through imitation, observation, and participation in social events. This form of education is not structured, does not have clearly defined goals, no definite curriculum, no trained teachers and no specific qualifications."[4] The

---

3. Kimizi, "Why has the Language of Instruction?" 9, 14.

4. Mugyenyi, *Aspects of Sociology*, 83, cf. Qorro, "Does Language of Instruction affect Quality?" 1.

INTRODUCTION

education held was more based on practical issues than theoretical ones. A boy was taught to make real things from available materials by looking at what his parent was doing. Likewise, the girl was instructed to craft real things from looking at what her mother was doing. As said earlier, this type of education was mostly informal, meaning that it was not based on formal classes, formal syllabuses, and formal promotions from one level to another; however, it was passed from one generation to the other through practical participation of the children to what was done by their elders.

We should "note that for African indigenous education, elders were the teachers, the fire place or under a tree was the classroom [sic!], and a whole range of subjects would be learnt, such as sports, domestic science, medicine, agriculture, blacksmithing and others. The methods of instruction were riddles, poems, folk story telling, mentoring, imitation, group work, and apprenticeship. The mothers, sisters, aunties, and grand mothers would teach girls while fathers, uncles, brothers, and grand fathers would teach boys."[5] In fact, this was the type of education that made life of the African people continue in the way it was. So, the view held by many Europeans who first came to Africa that Africans were uncivilized, pagan with no history and culture to perpetuate life was unquestionably wrong. These Europeans maintained that since Africans knew neither reading nor writing, they had no contents and methods to pass their education to the young. To such scholars, education in Africa meant Western civilization.

What education is as contrasted to the erroneous one held by European scholars? Education as defined by Sifuna & Otiende is "the process by which one generation transmits its culture to the succeeding generation or as a process by which people are prepared to live effectively and efficiently in their environment."[6] Qorro further defines education as being:

> a development process that often includes a particular understanding of the nature of knowledge. This understanding is given expression in a particular social or ideological context with its particular policy and implementation agendas. It is an expression of how human learning and development occurs and how they can be encouraged. Education is seen as a developmental process of change for the better in the interest of the society that designs it and the individual that receives it.[7]

5. Ibid., 83.
6. Sifuna & Otiende, *An Introductory History*, 129.
7. Qorro, "Does Language of Instruction affect Quality?" 1.

Taking both of the above definitions into account, we can say that Africans had as valuable education as the Europeans had; they had an education which was capable of being transmitted from one generation to another. Indeed, as the European formal education was, African indigenous education was also a process of passing the inherited knowledge, skills, cultural traditions, norms and values among the tribal members of a particular tribe, and from one generation to another in that tribe.

However, as it is to any other educational system, it had its weaknesses. One great weakness of African indigenous education was that it sorely relied on memory and oral tradition; it did not have any kind of books or written papers to keep the potential knowledge. Moreover, its scope was very limited. The knowledge was limited to a family, clan, or ethnic group level. It was not easily able to transcend to other parts outside the group that shared that particular knowledge.

As stated above, informal education was mostly based on participation in ongoing activities done by the elders (e.g., parents). This type of education was mostly provided in initiation ceremonies whereby children were taught adulthood. Ceremonies such as *Jando* (for boys) and *Unyago* (for girls) were formally known as being special for teaching mature children towards responsible adult life. Therefore, learning which is defined by Ngaroga, "as a process by which we acquire knowledge, from attitudes and develop skills that cannot be attributed to inherited behavior patterns or physical growth"[8] started a long time ago. It is a relatively permanent change in behavior which comes as a result of practice of an activity. It is not a European and Arabs' invention.

It is true that formal education was introduced in Africa by people from outside the continent. It started after the coming of Arabs who introduced *Madrasa*, whereby people were taught to read and write Arabic. The interest of Arabs was not education; it was business. So, the introduction of formal education meant teaching people to enable them read the Qur'an.

Formal education was more advanced by Europeans during the colonial era. It was strongly established during this colonial period with the aims of converting people into Christianity and preparing some Tanzanians who could help the colonial masters to realize their political, economic and social goals.[9] This means that the aim of the colonial education, as Mugyenyi rightly speaks, was "to civilize Africans, by changing their way of life,

---

8. Ngaroga, *Professional Studies*, 110.
9. Swilla, "Languages of Instruction," 2, cf. Mochiwa, "Kiswahili kwa kufundishia," 51.

INTRODUCTION

convert Africans to Christianity, provide elite education and make them submissive."[10] The colonial education meant to lead Tanzanians towards rejecting themselves and their cultural identity.

The current education system in Tanzania (the 2-7-4-2-3+ level system, i.e., pre-primary, primary, lower secondary, upper secondary, undergraduate, etc.) did not just emerge. It is a result of the various changes from the educational system which was developed by the European colonizers.[11] According to Mugyenyi, the Europeans, especially the British and missionaries in general, consolidated the early education in the levels of "catechists schools, bush schools/sub grade schools, elementary schools, central schools, high schools, technical and teacher training schools."[12] Despite the many problems which Europeans faced, such as diseases, rigidity of the African culture towards adapting changes, barriers in the language of communication with the natives, the education of the natives which took roots in the minds of people, lack of cooperation from the existing African leaders (chiefs), and people's inability to read and write (illiteracy),[13] yet they managed to streamline education in Tanganyika and fulfill their aims whose consequences are still visible within our current education system.[14]

Despite the many advantages of formal education introduced by Arabs and Europeans, it also had notable weaknesses. Formal education was mainly bookish and theoretical. Learners were emphasized to know how to read and write, but very little on how to do things practically. Moreover, formal education, with its curricular, syllabuses, and levels of promotion was accessible to few people who could manage to transcend those levels. Consequently, formal education was useful to those who established it (the Arabs and European colonizers) not the native Africans.

In a move from colonial education to more Afrcan oriented education after independence, something had to be done. On 05th February 1967 Tanzania adopted the *Ujamaa* and Education for Self-Reliance policy (ESR), championed by Julius K. Nyerere, the first president of the United Republic of Tanzania, emanating from the Arusha Declaration. This policy emphasized on the integration of work and agriculture. It also emphasized

---

10. Mugyenyi, *Aspects of Sociology*, 97, cf. Mochiwa, "Kiswahili kwa kufundishia," 51.

11. Ndalichako, "Analysis of Pupils' Difficulties," 69, cf. Mlay, "The Influence of the Language," 40–41.

12. Mugyenyi, *Aspects of Sociology*, 98.

13. Ibid.

14. Mochiwa, "Kiswahili kwa Kufundishia," 52–53.

on the expansion of primary schools making primary education a compulsory education for every child in Tanganyika. This was made possible through the abolition of school fees to enable as many children as possible to join primary schools.[15]

The above adopted educational system has passed through various changes until now. Several policies have been established and implemented apart from the above policy. These policies include: "The Education Ordinance (1969), Socialism and Rural Development (1968), Adult Education (1970), Villagization (1973), Musoma Resolution (1974), Universal Primary Education (UPE), (1977), Education and Training Policy (1995), The National Higher Education Policy (1995) and others."[16] The development and implementation of the above-mentioned policies indicate that Tanzania has passed through various educational, political, and communal reforms culminating to the current globalized context.

EDUCATION AND KISWAHILI LANGUAGE

Having outlined the history of education, this section discusses the dawn of Kiswahili language as a foundational language of instruction in Tanzania. In his article called "The Language of Instruction Issue in Tanzania," Telli argues: "For a country to be able to benefit from globalization through the free market of labor and capital, education should assume its role of preparing people to fit into the globalized and neoliberal world."[17] However, in order for education to accomplish this role, language is an important medium. Language is both a means of imparting knowledge to the intended audience and a tool for communication. This means that language can be taught as a language for communication or used for teaching knowledge to intended people.[18] Kiswahili, as a language—a means of communication, has been a wide spreading language both nationally and internationally and the most fluently spoken language in Tanzania. Therefore, it can be said that Kiswahili is second language to the mother tongues in almost all ethnic groups.[19]

15. Mugyenyi, *Aspects of Sociology*, 98–99.
16. Ibid., 99; cf. BAKITA, "BAKITA na Lugha ya Kufundishia," 1.
17. Telli, "The Language of Instruction," 11.
18. Qorro, "Matatizo ya Kutumia Kiingereza," 22.
19. Mulokozi, "Kiswahili as a National and International Language," cf. Ryanga, "The African Union," 5–6, 9–11; Msanjila, "Dhima ya Lugha ya Kiswahili," 16; Msanjila,

INTRODUCTION

The evolution of Kiswahili as a popular language in both normal communications and academic arenas came soon after Tanganyika's independence in 1961. However, the movement for its promotion started earlier, from 1930.[20] The language was primarily spoken in coastal areas of Tanzania because of the influence of the Arabs who mostly stayed in the coastal areas such as Dar es Salaam, Tanga, Bagamoyo, and Mtwara.[21] It was also used as medium of instruction in primary schools during the colonial period for Tanganyikan children together with English for European children and Gujarati language for Asian children.[22] On the one hand, during the German colonial rule (1886—1919), Kiswahili was emphasized in all stages of primary education and German was rarely taught in African schools.[23]

On the other hand, when the British occupied the country (from 1919 to 1961), Kiswahili was used to some stages of primary education and restricted to others. Kiswahili was used as a language of instruction from the first to the fifth year of children's study and gradually changed to English as language of instruction towards a full use of English as language of instruction in the sixth year. Different from the Germans who emphasized in Kiswahili as a language of instruction, the British emphasized in English. English became the language of the civilized and the educated. This led most people who knew English to hold a colonial mentality and view

---

"Kiswahili kutumika katika Umoja wa Afrika," 94. However, Ouane and Glanz define the mother tongue "as the language or languages of the immediate environment and daily interaction which 'nurture' the child in the first four years of life. Thus, the mother tongue is a language or languages with which the child grows up and of which the child has learned the structure before school." (Ouane & Glanz, *Why and How Africa should invest in African Languages*, 13.

20. Babaci-Wilhite & Geo-Jaja, "Localization of Instruction," 4; cf. Mtesigwa, "Utandawazi na Dhima ya Kiswahili," 69; Masudi, "The need for an Appropriate Medium," 34–6.

21. The word "*Swahili*" comes from the Arabic word "*suahel*" which means "coast" Therefore, *Kiswahili* means a coastal language which emerged because of the Arabs' business interactions with the natives in the coastal area who had their own coastal language since the first century CE. This means that the growth and expansion of Kiswahili from the coast to other parts of Tanganyika was possible through business, religion, and colonization (administration) (see Mtesigwa, "Utandawazi na Dhima ya Kiswahili," 69–72; cf. Khamisi, "Kiswahili ikiwa ni Lugha ya Kimataifa," 2).

22. Gran, "Language of Instruction, 8; cf. Swilla, "Languages of Instruction, 2; Kapoli "The effects of Interaction," 5; Mtesigwa, "Utandawazi na Dhima ya Kiswahili," 69.

23. See Masudi, "The need of an Appropriate Medium of Instruction," 33–34; cf. Kalmanlehto, "Mixed Domains,"17–18; Khamis, "Kiswahili ikiwa ni Lugha ya Kimataifa," 3; Sa, "Language Policy for Education," 3.

themselves as being more socially privileged than other Tanzanian fellows because they were able to secure white-collar jobs.

Moreover, the good pass of English was the guarantee for a student to be awarded an Oversees Cambridge School Certificate; and English was given more time in the schools' curricular than Kiswahili for all three types of schools based on race: African, Asian and European schools. For African schools, English language was taught by less qualified teachers, most of them not trained as teachers, but people of other professions.[24] During the British rule, English acquired a significant status in education, while Kiswahili was undermined.[25]

Mwalimu Julius K. Nyerere, the first President of the United Republic of Tanzania and other leaders of his time, found the necessity of using Kiswahili as a uniting language for the various ethnic groups within the country.[26] The language was announced as an official language to be used in all state and public functions in Tanganyika in 1962; and Nyerere himself addressed the Parliament in Kiswahili for the first time in December 1962. It was followed by the adoption of the policy of *Ujamaa* and Self-Reliance in 1967 which facilitated the gathering of people of different linguistic backgrounds under Kiswahili as a medium of communication, and the declaration in March 1967 that Kiswahili should be used as language of instruction in all primary schools within the whole United Republic of Tanzania.[27] Therefore, Kiswahili was emphasized in all sectors, public and private, as the official language of communication for state and public functions of the country, including the parliament. The then Vice President Rashid Kawawa announced Kiswahili a language of the Parliament on 4th July 1967.[28]

24. Cf. Swilla, "Languages of Instruction," 2; Brock-Utne & Holmasdottir, "Language Policies," 2; Kimizi, "Why has the Language of Instruction," 10–11; Kalmanlehto, "Mixed Domains," 18–19; Khamisi, "Kiswahili ikiwa ni Lugha ya Kimataifa," 3; Bwenge, "English in Tanzania," 169–170; Sa, "Language Policy for Education," 4.

25. In chapter two below, we will discuss more on English and its resurgence as a world language of communication.

26. Julius K. Nyerere was himself a teacher of Kiswahili in secondary schools before engaging with political affairs. He was also involved, with his fellow teachers, in the preparation of the Kiswahili curriculum for schools in the 1950s during the colonial regime (see Mwansoko, 2005:77).

27. Gran, "Language of Instruction," 8; Mulokozi, "Kiswahili as a National and International Language," 67–69; Brock-Utne & Holmasdottir, "Language Policies," 2; Kapoli, "The effects of Interaction," 2–5.

28. Dzahene-Quarshie, "The Language Policy," 29.

INTRODUCTION

The emphasis and promotion of Kiswahili as a Tanzanian *lingua franca*, that eventually became a national language in 1962, started even before independence (from 1930 as stated above). Karsten Legere quotes the words of J.W.T. Allen, the editor of *Kiswahili Journal* of 1959, two years before independence, who wrote about the efficacy and the forthcoming growth of Kiswahili language thus:

> During the past two decades the official attitude to Kiswahili has been more and more to disregard and despise it, to relegate it to the position of one of the many "vernaculars", whose use it is assumed will disappear with the spread and knowledge of English. During the same two decades the number of persons able to speak, read and write Swahili has increased enormously, and its value as a unifying factor is recognized by many in whose hands the future of East Africa may well lie. The later view is at least forcing some of the holders of the former view to reconsider their position, and there are signs of appreciation of the fact that no refusal to recognize it or assist it will suppress Swahili or arrest its growth as a modern practical vehicle for the exchange of thought between many millions of people who cannot in their generation learn English, and as a literary medium for that expression of beauty without which man cannot *survive. It is therefore with confidence that I prophesy the survival of Swahili for many years to come as a medium both of practical value in the modern world and for expressing the higher aspirations of the human mind.* That so little is done to further the study and development of the most important and widespread language of Africa...."[29]

Therefore, it will be noted in the course of this book that Allen's prophecy of 1959 before independence holds a considerable truth as currently the majority of Tanzanians and people from other East African countries can speak, read, write, and understand Kiswahili.

The evolution of Kiswahili as the official language of communication in Tanganyika, however, did not abolish the use of English, the language which the British colonizers imposed to Tanzanian systems of life, including the provision of colonial education. After independence, English remained a language of instruction in Secondary and Tertiary education systems.[30] Its

---

29. Legere, "Uwezeshwaji wa Kiswahili," 152–153, cf. Dzahene-Quarshie, "Language Policy," 28–29 (italics is in original).

30. Mgqwashu states clearly that most African countries south of the Sahara retained the languages of their colonizers as official languages after independence. Though some have elevated one or two local languages mostly spoken by people, the elevation is only to

13

retention is likely because of its international status to link higher education graduating students to the international academic guild, its being a language of business internationally linked with the current globalization and competition for labor market in the world, and the difficulty which the nation could face in translating all books and other teaching materials into English if it were to switch from Kiswahili to English.[31] Following these reasons, English is still left to be mostly a language for instruction in Tanzanian secondary schools, colleges and universities.

However, as it still holds on a foreign language as a language of instruction in some few pre-primary and primary, all secondary schools and university education, the Tanzanian government is still left with a question to answer: Which is more costly, translating books and other learning materials into Kiswahili, or leaving the majority of Tanzanians without a proper understanding of what they learn in secondary schools just internalizing the colonial imperial culture?[32]

In Tanzania, Kiswahili became the major means of instruction in Kindergarten and Primary school levels of education soon after independence. It seems, Nyerere and the current leadership aimed at promoting Kiswahili as the means of communication at all levels of education (Kindergarten, Primary schools and Vocational trainings, and even higher learning levels of education) instead of using the language of the colonizers which connoted the adoption of the culture and identity of the colonizers and their imperialism, which would further lead to internalizing their attitudes and

---

being a national language not being official language. For example Kenya and Tanzania, whose legally recognized official language is English, have elevated *Kiswahili* to being a national language (see Mgqwashu, "Language and Postcolonial Condition," 300–301). In the case of Tanzania, *Kiswahili* is not recognized by the national constitution leading to forfeiting the rights of most Tanzanian who understand *Kiswahili*, as Laws are written in English and High Court activities are conducted in English (see Gawasike, "Lugha ya Kiswahili," 73–74). However, Legere quotes the words of the first president of Tanganyika emphasizing the retention of English language just after independence saying: "*Kiingereza ni Kiswahili cha Dunia. Ni makosa kukiachia Kiingereza kikafa. Kukiachia ni ujinga, siyo uzalendo.*" [Literally: English is the Kiswahili of the World. It is a mistake to let English die. To let it die is foolishness; it is not patriotism.] (Legere, "Marehemu Julius Kambarage Nyerere," 55). These words reflect the mentality which most leaders of African countries had just after independence.

31. Marwa, "Tanzanians' Language of Instruction"; Telli, "The Language of Instruction," 13; Kapoli, "The effects of Interaction," 2–7.

32. Kimizi, "Why has the Languages of Instruction?" 76; cf. Gawasike, "Lugha ya Kiswahili,".70.

INTRODUCTION

power.³³ Moreover, as Babaci-Wilhite and Geo-Jaja say, "In Tanzania, the policy of switching from Kiswahili to English midway through the schooling process gives the impression that Kiswahili is inferior to English and that the local language is somehow inadequate in engaging with complex concepts."³⁴ Certainly, this notion is not true as we will illustrate in the course of this book.

Godfrey Telli asserts that one important reason for promoting Kiswahili as a language of instruction in all levels of education is that "learners can actively participate in knowledge creation if they are allowed to use the language they understand very well, which, in most cases, is the language they usually speak in their day-to-day life."³⁵ This means that the ability of students to understand what they learn and use it in various sectors after they graduate is directly proportional to the language of instruction used in their process of learning.

Following the great hegemony of Kiswahili as Tanzania's *lingua franca*, it was the plan of the country that Kiswahili should be used as a language of instruction in all levels of education—primary, secondary and tertiary education. Attempts towards using Kiswahili as a language of instruction were initially "made in 1972 following a conference held in the Tanzanian town of Dodoma by heads of the ruling party (then TANU), the Government and the University of Dar es Salaam."³⁶ Afterwards, the *Cultural Policy of 1997* (*Sera ya Utamaduni 1997*) acknowledged the weakness of using foreign languages as languages of instructions when it states clearly:

> Katika mfumo rasmi wa Elimu, Kiswahili kinatumika kama lugha ya kufundishia katika elimu ya awali, msingi, mafunzo ya Cheti cha Elimu ya Ualimu, na elimu ya watu wazima. Kuanzia ngazi ya elimu ya sekondari hadi elimu ya juu Kiingereza ndiyo lugha ya kufundishia. Utaratibu huu umedhoofisha lugha ya Kiswahili pamoja na maendeleo ya elimu, sayansi na tekinolojia nchini. Jitihada za serikali yoyote ile ya kujenga umoja na mshikamano wa kitaifa kwa kutumia Mfumo Rasmi wa Elimu ambao hautumii lugha ya taifa kama lugha ya kufundishia zinasababisha siyo tu uharibifu wa urithi wa utamaduni wa nchi hiyo, bali pia zinachangia katika kuleta na kuendeleza umaskini na mtafaruku katika jamii. Hali hii inatokana na kiwango cha chini cha wananchi walio wengi cha

---

33. Kimizi, "Why has the Languages of Instruction?" 70.
34. Babaci-Wilhite & Geo-Jaja, "Localization of Instruction," 11.
35. Telli, "The Language of Instruction," 10.
36. Kapoli, The effects of Interaction, 6.

kuelewa, kuzungumza na kuandika lugha za kigeni zinazotumiwa kufundishia. Kama tutaendelea kufundisha kwa lugha ya Kiingereza sayansi na tekinolojia ambayo tunaihitaji sana kwa maendeleo ya taifa letu katika karne ya ishirini na moja itaendelea kuwa haki ya watu wachache wanaofahamu Kiingereza. [Literal translation: In the current official Educational system, Kiswahili is used as a language of instruction in pre-primary, primary Certificate of Teachers' Education, and adult education. From the level of secondary education to higher education, English is the language of instruction. This system has mostly weakened Kiswahili language, the development of education and science and technology in the country. The initiatives of any government to consolidate national unity and solidarity by using an Official System of Education which does not use its national language as a language of instruction causes not only the destruction of the cultural heritage of that country, but also contributes towards perpetuating poverty and misunderstandings within the community. This happens because of the low ability of citizens to understand, speak, and write foreign languages used for instruction. If we will continue to teach using English language science and technology, which we urgently need for the development of our nation in the twenty first century, will remain to be the right of the few minority who understand English.][37]

However, it is stated thus in the Cultural Policy (Policy Statements): "A Special programme to enable the use of Kiswahili as a medium of instruction in education and training at all levels shall be designed and implemented."[38]

The move towards an implementation of this plan was done thorough the introduction of responsible bodies such as BAKITA (the National Kiswahili Council) with the responsibility of promoting and developing Kiswahili in all areas of Tanzanian lives, the Institute for Kiswahili Research at the University of Dar es Salaam, and circular sent in 1969 ordering that Kiswahili and *Siasa* (political science) subjects should be taught in Kiswahili.[39] However, the development of Kiswahili as a language of instruction in higher learning institutions is yet to be realized because of what proponents of the use of English call: the possible disadvantages the country will encounter if it will be opted as a language of instruction—especially the ones related to costs for the transition—despite the suggestions provided by Jackson Makweta's

37. URT, *Sera ya Utamaduni*, 19; cf. URT, *Sera ya Elimu*, 37–38.
38. URT, *Cultural Policy Statements*, 3.
39. Gran, "Language of Instruction" cf. Babaci-Wilhite &Geo-Jaja, "Localization of Instruction," 5.

INTRODUCTION

Presidential Commission for Education of 1980, which suggested that Kiswahili should be used as a language of instruction for secondary schools from 1985 and in universities and colleges from 1992.[40] For a long time there have been unrealized endeavors towards the Tanzania's reform on the language of instruction more than the instruction that Kiswahili should be used for teaching Kiswahili and *Siasa* subjects. It stopped there until when *siasa* was also removed from the curriculum in 1993 and civics subject, taught in English, reinstituted in the secondary schools curricular instead. The current model of language of instruction for the various levels of education in Tanzania is as indicated in the diagram below.

40. Ibid., 10.

A Sketch of Education System in Tanzania Mainland

Postgraduate Studies
English is LoI, Kiswahili is LoI for Kiswahili Studies

↑

University Level Education (Undergraduate 3 Years)
English is LoI, Kiswahili is LoI for Kiswahili Studies

↑ ↑ ↑

Under NECTA
Teacher Education (Diploma 2 Years)
(English is LoI, Kiswahili taught as Subject)

Under NACTE
Diploma Education (2 Years)
(English is LoI)

↑ ↑

Under NECTA
Advanced Secondary Education (2 Years)
English is LoI, Kiswahili is taught as a subject

↑

Under NECTA
Teacher Education Grade IIIa (Certificate)
(Kiswahili is LoI, English is taught as a subject)

Under NACTE
Certificate Level Education (1 Year)
(English is LoI)

↑ ↑

Under NECTA
Ordinary Secondary Education (4 Years)
(English is LoI, Kiswahili is taught as a Subject)

↓

Under VETA
Vocational Education
(Kiswahili and English as Languages of Instruction)

↑

Under NECTA
Primary Education (7 Years)
(Kiswahili is LoI for Government Schools; English is LoI for the few Private Schools)

↑

Under NECTA
Pre-Primary Education (2 Years)
(Kiswahili is LoI for the Majority Pre-Primary Schools, and English is taught as a subject. English is LoI for the few English Medium Schools)

Source: Authors' own Sketch

INTRODUCTION

The above diagram indicates the four main levels of education in the Tanzanian educational system operating currently. The first level is the "Primary Level" which comprises of two parts: the "Pre-primary (kindergarten) and Primary" educational levels. The kindergarten prepares children of 5 to 6 years for joining primary schools. Normally, Primary Schools admit children of not less than 7 years; and Primary School studies last for seven years. As a compulsory level of study, primary level education lays a foundation for children's cultural and ethical orientations towards being self-reliant and responsible Tanzanian citizens. Moreover, it prepares them for secondary education, vocational training, and for taking various normal responsibilities in society.[41]

The second level according to the above diagram is "Secondary Education." This level of education is also divided into two: the Ordinary Level (forms 1–4) and advanced level (forms 5–6). As indicated in the diagram above, students completing the first level (form 1–4) are expected to join the next level of secondary education (forms 5–6), join Vocational or professional trainings, join Certificate Level education, or join the majority work force of the country. Those students completing Advanced Level education (forms 5–6) have only three options: joining Diploma Education, joining University Education, or joining the general work force of the country. As Msuya states, "The goals of secondary education in Tanzania are to provide best knowledge, intuitive minds and basic foundations for higher education that will create a competent citizen who can suit for national development. . . . "[42] Hence, having completed the second part of secondary education, the student is expected to have an experience of six years of English as language of instruction for all subjects of study to enable that student to pursue University education. The student is also expected to have education that makes him/her a competent citizen. The question here is whether students attain educational competency which is appropriate to their level with the use of English, a foreign language as LoI.

The third level is Tertiary education. In this level the student is channeled into certificates, diplomas and degrees. As indicated in the above diagram, Secondary education usually leads to tertiary education. Students completing form four are expected to join in non-degree training colleges

41. Ndalichako, "Analysis of Pupils' Difficulties," 69–70; Sodhi, *Textbook of Comparative Education*, 70–109; Ngimbudzi, "Job Satisfaction among Secondary School Teachers," 26.

42. Msuya, "Exploring Levels of Job Satisfaction," 10; Sodhi, *Textbook of Comparative Education*, 111–162.

where certificates are awarded. Those completing the second part of secondary education may join universities for pursuing degree studies, or join non-degree training for diploma studies depending on their performances. The main purpose of tertiary education in Tanzania is to orient graduating individuals into the world of work. It prepares them for taking middle and high level professional responsibilities as work forces in various sectors within the country. The question here is similar to that of the previous level—whether students attain educational competency which is appropriate to their level by using English, a foreign language, as LoI.

Kiswahili, being the main language of instruction at lower levels of education means that children master it fully as they complete their studies. This is mostly the case when children complete standard seven. As it will be noted in this research, children who begin secondary studies tend to turn to Kiswahili in order to understand the English-taught content in both classes and individual group discussions. Researches and our own experience as teachers show that, in some cases, teachers are obliged to speak Kiswahili to clarify issues when teaching in order to make students understand the content of what is being taught.[43] This obligation to turn to Kiswahili indicates that Kiswahili could be the most favorable language of instruction because its roots begin at the early life of the child, and is the language which the child masters well besides the mother tongue.

However, Swilla clearly states the contradictions that exist to the government's option to use Kiswahili as language of instruction: first, "while the government statements maintain that Swahili is the LoI of primary education, English has been legalized as the LoI in private primary schools."[44] Second, the government which emphasizes Kiswahili as the language of instruction in primary schools has itself provided the English curriculum to private English medium primary schools. It is also the one which has been preparing and administering national English primary school leaving examinations for private English medium primary schools. The question is: Why should the Tanzanian government prepare the English curriculum for the minority private primary schools; while it itself continues to emphasize on Kiswahili as a medium of instruction to all its primary schools attended by the majority pupils in rural and urban places? In other words, why leave the English medium curriculum to the private sector, if not promoting elitism—producing the majority Kiswahili speakers and minority English

---

43. See Marwa, "Tanzania's Language of Instruction Policy."
44. Swilla, "Languages of Instruction," 6; URT, *Education and Training Policy*, 35.

speakers who boast of being more educated because of their knowledge of English, an international language?[45]

To us, the above contradictions and ambivalences indicate a gradual shift from the national plan of Kiswahili being the language of instruction in primary and vocational training levels of education towards English, in a similar way Kiswahili was removed in teaching *siasa* subject in secondary schools in 1993. However, we agree with Kimizi when he quotes Kiango saying, "'To plan is to choose, and for any decision that is made, there is a need to be able to predict how it will affect our countries [sic!] in future'. Sticking to this logic, therefore, the Tanzanian government should plan to choose the LOI based on whose language; is chosen for whose benefit; and in whose interest; instead of remaining ambivalent."[46]

COMMUNITY SECONDARY SCHOOLS IN TANZANIA

After discussing the boldness of Kiswahili language, this part introduces the history of community secondary schools in Tanzania. Certainly, community secondary schools are not a new phenomenon in Tanzania. It was established some years back with special objectives. Here we provide a brief enlightenment to all education stakeholders on the origin of community secondary schools and their objectives. Undoubtedly, the establishment of community schools is one of the major educational reforms to secondary education in Tanzania during the 1980s and 1990s.

The 1995 Education and Training Act No.10 defined community secondary schools as those schools owned by the local community, or owned by an institution on behalf of the community.[47] The community of a particular place is the one which determines the type of school they would want it to be, the place to locate their school, and the control of teaching and administrative affairs of the school. Hence, community secondary schools in Tanzania are basically established by people at the Ward, Division, or District levels before they are reported to the central government for supply of teaching and learning materials, teaching work force, or teaching staff and administrators.[48]

---

45. Bwenge, "English in Tanzania," 175.
46. Kimizi, "Why has the Language of Instruction?" 78–79.
47. Muganda, et al., "Introduction to Education."
48. Ngimbudzi, "Job Satisfaction among Secondary School Teachers," 20.

At first, community secondary schools in Tanzania were implemented in 1970s when the government decided to nationalize private secondary schools for the aim of abolishing racial discrimination left by colonialists by that time. Private secondary schools were not for all people with all levels of economic status. They were for the few elites, those who were able to pay for them.[49] Telli clearly affirms: "Technically, private schools in Tanzania are mainly for the few elite members of the population and high level government officials due to high cost of enrolment and other numerous inhibitive fees."[50]

The second implementation took place in 1980s and 1990s; this period experienced further changes in the history of community secondary education in Tanzania. The first major change was the re-introduction of community secondary schools as a response to the extraordinary increase of social demand for secondary education following the implementation of the Universal Primary Education (UPE),[51] the implementation which created unparalleled social demands for secondary education.

The government issued a circular in 1984 to initiate a ten year program for the expansion of secondary education.[52] The program became implemented effectively in 1986 and was to be completed by 1995 with the construction of 79 secondary schools which were to be distributed in such a way that each region was to build three schools. Essentially, community secondary schools are government schools with divided responsibilities between local communities on one hand and the central government on the other.[53]

As just stated, community secondary schools are planned and run by the community in which the children live. These community secondary

---

49. Telli, "The Language of Instruction"; Tibategeza, "Implementation of Bilingual Education"; Swilla, "Language of Instruction."

50. Telli, "The Language of Instruction," 11.

51. Universal Primary Education (UPE) was one of the United Nations Development goals whose purpose was to ensure that by the year 2015 children everywhere in the world equally achieved primary education, both boys and girls. In Tanzania, the UPE was realized as a national policy by the year 1977. This policy led to the introduction of Teachers Grade IIIB (these were standard seven who underwent training in Teachers colleges for three to four years) and Grade IIIC (these were recruited to the teaching profession just after completing standard seven and attending a short course) in order to meet the demand of teachers in Primary schools (see John, "What is the Difference," 62 footnote 11; Komba & Nkumbi, "Teacher Professional Development, 68).

52. Muganda, et al., "Introduction to Education."

53. Muganda, et al., "Introduction to Education."

INTRODUCTION

schools ensure access to education for children who would not otherwise have had the opportunity of attending school elsewhere in the country. However, this does not mean that students who are admitted do not have the qualifications which are similar to those admitted to government schools. They have all the necessary qualifications, but are not admitted to government schools because of lack of space. Hence, the permission of the state that community initiatives be involved in the provision of education was based on the fact that space in government schools was not proportional to the number of qualified students completing standard seven each year. The introduction of community secondary schools is a government strategy to ensure that all qualified students attain secondary education in the country.

Community secondary schools are also established in nearby countries such as Kenya. Community schools under this category in Kenya are called "*Harambee Schools*;" and in Tanzania, they are called "*Shule za Kata*" (Ward Schools) because of its nature of community involvement, mobilization, and contribution made to plant and advance them. Definitely, one cannot deny that it was a good idea to establish these schools.[54]

However, it looks like students in these secondary schools face many problems unlike those in Government and private (or religious owned) secondary schools. Together with other problems, students in these schools perform poorly at Form Four formative and summative examinations as compared to their counterparts. Therefore, this study will focus on assessing the effectiveness and shortcomings of the use of English in community secondary schools to both teachers and students.

From this sub-section, the we have discussed the Government efforts to improve education in the country. The Government initiated several education programs for the purpose of ensuring that the youth of this country are able to acquire "quality education"[55] to enable them be productive

---

54. URT, "Education Sector Development," vi; cf. Onsumu et al. *Community Schools*, 13–14; Wamalwa, Adika & Kevogo, "Multilingualism and Language Attitudes," 57.

55. The concepts of *quality education* and *quality of education* are used interchangeably in this book. However, according to Qorro, these concepts are slightly different. She defines the two concepts thus: "quality education refers to the state of education a society strives to attain; while quality of education focuses on quality that we strive to improve." (Qorro, "Does Language of Instruction affect Quality?" 1) In Tanzania, the "quality of education" provided in all three types of schools, government, community and private secondary schools, will depend mainly on the goals set by the Tanzanian government (see URT, *Education and Training Policy*, 6). However, Qorro further notes, "Quality education is the kind of education that gives learners the ability to learn and discuss abstract ideas, liberates learners' minds from ignorance, opens up new perspectives and

members of society. The establishment of community secondary schools is one of the Government's efforts which aimed at ensuring the increased population of Tanzanian youth acquiring secondary education in their local areas. Community secondary schools are now at every Ward of the country; and hence, they facilitate the accessibility of secondary education to children around them.

PROBLEM AND OBJECTIVES

Despite the resurgence of community secondary schools in Tanzania (at least every Ward) as discussed above, the question is whether the education provided in these schools correspond to what students are supposed to attain at this educational level as they excel in the educational system. This section states unambiguously the problem facing the current Tanzanian education system which most likely leads to poor performance in community secondary schools and the major objectives for conducting this study. Formerly, the education system of Tanzania required pupils at primary school level to study seven subjects. At the national standard seven examinations, pupils do five subjects which are Mathematics, English, Science, Kiswahili and social studies—which include History, Geography and Civics. To the Swahili medium primary schools, which are for the majority Tanzanian children, all the subjects mentioned are taught in Kiswahili except English.[56] However, Kiswahili is not the language which most pupils, especially those in rural areas, speak after they are born. After they are born, most of them are taught mother tongues, especially in rural areas where the majority Tanzanians live. It should be born in mind that Tanzania has more than 120 different mother tongues spoken throughout the country.[57] This means

---

extends their horizons by widening frontiers of knowledge. Quality education requires that learners take an active part in knowledge creation through critical thinking, discussion, dialogue, asking questions and solving problems." (Qorro, "Does Language of Instruction affect Quality?" 3)

56. Bikongoro shows that by 2014 there were 15,884 Kiswahili medium primary schools which had 808,286 candidates for the National Examination; while there were 663 English medium primary schools which had 24,826 candidates for the National Examination (see Bikongoro, "The Relevance of the Language, 2). These figures indicate that most children in Tanzania attend *Kiswahili* medium primary schools and only a few of them attend English medium primary schools.

57. Marwa, "Tanzania's Language of Instruction"; Senkoro, "Language of Instruction," 7; Kimizi, "Why has the Language of Instruction," 11.

that, in primary schools, most pupils, especially those in rural areas, are being transformed from using their mother tongues to master the national language (Kiswahili). This is the first drastic change of language to pupils as they grow in the Tanzanian education system.

There is a second drastic change when pupils complete standard seven and move to secondary school (form one to four) whereby all subjects are now taught in English except Kiswahili. This abrupt change from fully Kiswahili-based to fully English-based teaching makes most students unable to understand what they are taught, and begin struggling to master the English language vocabularies in each subject taught instead of struggling to understand the content of what they are taught. As Person rightly notes, the transition from entire Kiswahili use in most primary schools to entire English language use in secondary schools is like sending students to the sea fishing without fishing-nets with them. Students complete studies in primary schools with high knowledge, but fail to use it when in secondary school to create more knowledge because of the language barrier.[58] They go to secondary schools without a fishing-net, i.e., without the knowledge of English language as a tool for teaching and learning in secondary schools. Will they catch any fish? As it will be vivid in this study, this is hardly possible!

Mulokozi states the impossibility to fish without a proper fishing-net more clearly when he writes:

> *Tokeo mojawapo la sera hii ya lugha mbili [Kiswahili na Kiingereza]ni kwamba ingawa katika shule nyingi za sekondari walimu na wanafunzi wanatumia Kiswahili katika kuelewana wanalazimika kuandaa madondoo ya masomo na mitihani kwa lugha ya Kiingereza. Hivyo, wapo wanafunzi wengi wanaoyamudu masomo yao kwa Kiswahili lakini wanashindwa mtihani kwa sababu hawawezi kujibu maswali kwa lugha ya Kiingereza, na hawaruhusiwi kujibu kwa lugha ya Kiswahili."* [Literally: One of the results of this two-language policy [Swahili and English] is that despite that students use Kiswahili to communicate in most secondary schools, yet they are obliged to prepare their study notes and answer examinations in English language. Hence, there are many students who can manage their studies in Kiswahili language but fail examinations because they are not able to answer questions in English language used, and are not allowed to answer such questions in Kiswahili language][59]

---

58. Person, "It's Like going Fishing," 47–48.
59. Mulokozi, "Baadhi ya Vipingamizi vya Kiutawala," 14.

It should be remembered that most of these students can hardly make a single grammatically correct sentence when they come from primary schools where all subjects were taught in Kiswahili to secondary school.[60] Hence, it is likely that one of the causes of students' failures at Form Four examinations in community secondary schools is contributed by their unfamiliarity with English language as a language of teaching and learning. The transition from mother tongue to Kiswahili then to English creates a difficulty for students from majority Swahili medium primary schools to master English language, which is the key language of teaching and learning in secondary and tertiary education.[61] This is the major problem facing students at community secondary schools where this study was done.

This difficulty does not end with pupils who complete primary education, and neither are they the ones who caused this lack of understanding the taught content at secondary schools. Most students who move from primary to secondary education level have a bad foundation of English because teachers who teach them also have a bad foundation of the language from their primary, secondary, and teacher training college levels.[62] This trend indicates that the problem of English proficiency that eventually leads to poor teachers' delivery of quality education for students' use in creating knowledge is systemic, not individual one.

Moreover, the transition from simply understood native languages commonly spoken in the homes to a more complex foreign language not commonly spoken in the homes most likely hinders learners from grasping the required cultural issues.[63] Senkoro makes this point clear that since English is imposed abruptly to students who have been studying the baseline ideas for a long time and using the native language, it hinders the anchoring of the baseline ideas studied; and in so doing, English becomes an enslaving language, both culturally and intellectually, instead of liberating children who attend schools.[64]

English language makes students internalize it as a hegemonic language equating it with being educated while despising their Kiswahili as

---

60. See Telli, "The Language of Instruction."

61. Marwa, "Tanzania's Language of Instruction"; Telli, "The Language of Instruction"; Senkoro, "Language of Instruction," 6; Bikongoro, "The Relevance of the Language, 4–7.

62. BAKITA, "BAKITA na Lugha," 4.

63. Cf. Neke, "English in Tanzania," 38; Rugemarira, "Theoretical and Practical Challenges," 68–69.

64. Senkoro, "Language of Instruction," 16.

INTRODUCTION

a native language. Stephen Mugeta Neke clarifies this point thus: "English is privileged by language policy to be used in the most prestigious social, educational and economic domains leading people to equate it with education, knowledge, civilization, and development. It has been argued that English is equated with good quality education while Kiswahili is said to be the language of 'Education for Self-Reliance (ESR)', 'Ujamaa', politics, adult literacy, poor quality education and poverty."[65] Consequently, English divides Tanzanians into two classes of people: those who are considered to be educated few (those who know a little beat of English and studied in English in pre-primary schools, primary schools, secondary schools, colleges and universities—the elite group) and the non-educated majority (those who do not know English and have studied up to primary level education using Kiswahili—the non-elite majority).[66] The question here is whether this divisive tendencies and attitudes should continue to be encouraged in a free country like Tanzania which constitutionally promotes the equality of all human beings.

The attitude of despising Kiswahili, according to Mulokozi, is caused by what he called in Kiswahili *kasumba mbaya* (evil mentality) towards it which causes the "erosion of self-confidence among Tanzanians, especially the youth and the elite, reading [sic!] to a resurgence of a slavish, aping mentality and practice"[67] in regard to the use of their own language. Mulokozi further adds that *kasumba mbaya* (evil mentality) has accelerated the "admiration and worship of foreign things, including the huge Japanese cars called *shangingis*, and foreign cultural manifestations, including music, cinema, and videos, dress, technology and language."[68] The evil mentality (*kasumba*), according to Mulokozi has caused Africans to despise even the important elements of their culture and being.

Mulokozi further states: "*katika dunia ya leo ni Mwafrika pekee anayeikataa rangi yake na kujitahidi kuichubua ili kupunguza weusi, ni Mwafrika pekee anayekataa lugha yake, dini yake ya asili, mavazi, tekinolojia, hata majina ya kabila au taifa lake, na kukimbilia kuiga mambo ya wengine.*" [Literary: In the world of today, it is the African alone who rejects the own

65. Neke, "English in Tanzania," x; Rugemarira, "Theoretical and Practical Challenges," 68–69; Mochiwa, "Kiswahili kwa Kufundishia," 52–53; and Dzahene-Quarshie, "Language Policy," 29.

66. Bwenge, "English in Tanzania," 175.

67. Mulokozi, "Kiswahili as a National and International Language," 71; cf. Mulokozi, "Baadhi ya Vipingamizi vya Kiutawala," 17.

68. Mulokozi, "Kiswahili as National and International Language," 71.

color of skin and struggles to change it in order to reduce its blackness; it is the African alone who rejects the own language, the own traditional religion, the own technology, and even the own tribal names or national names, and rushes on imitating other people's affairs].[69] In doing that, *kasumba* teaches people to be someone else, not pure Africans. This study intends to assess the extent to which the use of English is a barrier to teaching and learning processes in community secondary schools in Tanzania.

Another issue arising from the abrupt switching of language from Kiswahili used by most primary schools to English in secondary schools, colleges and universities stands between the type of people prepared to provide service (the minority who study using English language) and the type of people to whom service will be provided (the majority of Tanzanians). English is not the language spoken or used in normal services of the majority Tanzanians; yet, it is the language taught to minority Tanzanians who after completing studies become servants of the majority Kiswahili speakers in various sectors. This difference in terms of language between the majority served and the minority serving creates an unnecessary cultural and behavioral gap between them. Moreover, the use of English, a foreign language, makes most of those graduating from secondary schools, colleges and universities unfit to serve Tanzanians, but fit to serve people of other nations who use English as a means of communication.[70] This situation may be one of the possible reason as to why most educated people in Africa, and Tanzania in particular, move to other countries in search for greener pastures.

Following the stated and described problem in this part, the book has two main objectives: first, it assesses the impacts brought by the use of English language as a language for teaching and learning to students overall acquisition of the required academic content in community secondary schools in Tanzania. Second, it makes a case that Kiswahili is the appropriate language of instruction from primary to higher learning institutions in Tanzania. Some specific objectives will enable us reach the above two objectives. Such specific objectives include assessing the current academic performance in these schools; examining students' and teachers' proficiency in speaking, writing, and reading English; determining the reasons for their inability to use English efficiently in their learning process, and surveying Kiswahili and

---

69. Mulokozi, "Baadhi ya Vipingamizi vya Kiutawala," 16, for a similar situation in Namibia, see Chavez, "Rights in Education," 193.

70. Qorro, "Matatizo ya Kutumia Kiingereza," 23.

its legacy in Tanzania. Generally, we want to assess whether English, a foreign language spoken by a very few people in Tanzania (5 percent of Tanzanians), should continue to be used as a medium of instruction in secondary schools. It is worthwhile to say that, this study helps to establish scientific answers in regard to strengths and weaknesses of using English as a teaching and learning medium in community secondary school in Tanzania as other previous researches have done about this language.[71]

SIGNIFICANCE OF THE BOOK

Any meaningful research study must have significance to different stakeholders. This study which deals with the use of English as a teaching and learning medium in community secondary schools has several benefits. The findings are useful to different educational stakeholders: first, they are useful to educational policy-makers. Based on the findings and recommendations given, policy-makers may decide to review secondary school policies and guidelines in order to improve the sector. In addition, the government may opt to have a close look at community secondary schools in the country so as to ensure quality education they provide to Tanzanian children.

Second, the study creates awareness to community secondary schools in the study area, in the country, in Africa, and the world at large in regard to the effectiveness and shortcomings of the quality of education given by using a foreign and not fully known language, such as the English language which is even not a mother tongue, as a medium of communication leaving aside the mother tongue and fully known languages such as Kiswahili. This awareness is expected to provide morale and act as a positive impetus for students and teachers to work hard so as to master the foreign language used for teaching and learning; if there is a necessity to continue with it.

Third, it is our expectations that even the Ministry of Education and Vocational Training (MoEVT), which is responsible for ensuring quality education in the country, will be fully aware on what is happening in

---

71. A considerable number of researches have been conducted about this Language of instruction issue in Tanzania since 1980s. The effects have been analyzed, discussed, and recommendations provided by researchers on what should be done. However, as Qorro argues in her article, most of the findings of these researches have not been heeded by policy-makers. This book is a contribution to the endeavors of researchers to present the real situation of how the policy on language of instruction has been inadequate and the need for a better decision on the language of instruction for students to benefit from the knowledge provided to them (See Qorro, "Language of Instruction in Tanzania," 1).

community Secondary schools and take deliberate efforts to rescue the situation by developing guidelines, laws and other policies in order to improve the quality of education in the country. Moreover, the Ministry, through its organs, will be able to monitor and evaluate the progress of the sector. The findings of this study will help them to know what has to be closely monitored and evaluated for efficient and effective provision of education. And more important, the findings will make the ministry have proper decisions on whether to continue with English as LoI or decline it in this time whereby the reputation of Kiswahili greatly increases nationally and internationally.

Fourth, the study will create awareness to parents with children both in primary and community secondary schools. Parents will understand the strengths and weaknesses of their children having little knowledge of English because of the mother tongues taught at homes, and the fact that currently English is used as a major medium of communication at secondary schools. This awareness may help parents to rethink on how to help their children grown in mother tongues have better performances and successful shifts to Kiswahili and to English as they move from one level to another in the current Tanzanian educational system. Moreover, it will enlighten parents on the fact that equating knowledge of English with being educated is nonsensical. It is a mentality (*kasumba*) that keeps them slaves of their colonial masters.

Fifth, the study will also provoke other researchers to think more about the use of English in community, private and government secondary schools, and possibly conduct more research works on these areas. To our view, education is one of the fragile areas, if not the most fragile of all, because the nation will not have enough skilled personnel in various sectors if many students will not acquire the required level of educational competency to enable them perform at secondary level studies adequately. Hence, the question of education and its policies requires close attention from all stakeholders in the country.

Chapter 2

Looking Back
Review of Related Literatures

"If I have seen further it is by standing on the shoulders of giants."
—Sir Isaac Newton (1642—1727)

INTRODUCTION

Having introduced the background of the problem, stated the problem, and showed the importance of the book in the previous chapter, this chapter examines what is already known about the problem through reviewing literatures relating to the topic of the book. Scholars agree that literature review has to do with a comprehensive survey of what has been done to what one wants to do. It is a survey of different resent, relevant, and prominent books, journals and articles relating to the problem under study to envisage the significance of the problem in the topic, the theoretical perspective that informs the study, and how the proposed study fits to the existing knowledge.[1] This is what Isaac Newton (1642—1727) calls "standing on the shoulders of the giants." Doing literature review is searching for the known knowledge in order to construct the new one basing on the

---

1. Mligo, *Introduction to Research Methods*, 108-110; Mligo, *Doing Effective Fieldwork*, 65; Machi & McEvoy, *The Literature Review*, 4; Mouton, *How to Succeed*, 86-91; Vyhmeister, *Quality Research Papers*, 209-212; Aveyard, *Doing Literature Review*, 5; Hart, *Doing Literature Review*.

known one. Therefore, literatures review is more intriguing to write, and its importance is ranked in a similar weight with the report itself because it determines who are the giants in whose shoulders one wants to see further.

Following the above understanding, the review of literatures in this book will be organized in three levels, namely: global, continental and country levels. The second subsection of this chapter provides an overview of the use of English as a teaching and learning medium in general, the third discusses the use of English as a teaching and learning medium at a global level, and the fourth reviews literatures on the use of English as a teaching and learning medium at continental level. In addition, the fifth section discusses literatures on the use of English as a teaching and learning medium at a national level, the sixth section is about some best practices for teaching and learning using other languages, the seventh section identifies the research gap, and eventually, the eighth section concludes the chapter by summarizing the main concepts discussed. This chapter argues that the use of English as a language for teaching and learning posses challenges not only to Tanzanian students whose Kiswahili has been the prominent language of communication, but also to other countries which use English as a language of teaching and learning while having other popularly used native languages.

ENGLISH AS A MEDIUM FOR TEACHING AND LEARNING

The English language has a complex status in today's world. For some people, it is the first language. For some, it may be learned at school, and be essential for their academic and professional success. Yet for others, English may represent a subject that they are required to study in school, but for which they have no immediate need. In addition, English means different things to people in different parts of the world. For some, it may arouse positive feelings as the language of popular culture, the media, and social networking. For many developing countries, like Tanzania, English is mostly associated with colonialism and cultural imperialism because it represents a particular culture that is different from the indigenous cultures of those countries.[2] Moreover, the language may also be associated with

---

2. We cannot neglect the fact that there are researches done in Tanzania which show that students find English as being a suitable Language of instruction. Such researches include those of Nyamubi, 2016 and Kadeghe, 2010. However, as we will demonstrate throughout this book, these researches are fewer as compared to the opinion of the majority researches which find the use of English language as LoI to be more challenging.

elitism or social and economic status because, in most cases, it is used by coercion from the economically powerful nations that use English as their first language. As a symbol of cultural imperialism, it ruins people's sense of belonging to their own cultural tradition, being forced to imitate the culture of those powerful nations whose language they use. In that case, people's self and national identities are ruined severely.[3]

Today, English has a unique status as a consequence of the role it plays around the world and its function as an 'international' or 'world language'. It has been described as the world's *first spoken International language*. It should be remembered that people in countries like Australia, Canada, the United States and Great Britain use it as their first language, and is used as one of the official languages by almost 26 African countries as Plonski, Teferrra and Brady report in the abstract of their article:

> At least 26 African countries list English as one of their official languages. Most recently Rwanda, long a French-speaking country, has switched to English as an official language. Burundi and Gabon are switching from French to English, and South Sudan is adopting English. The use of English as an official language in schools, universities, and government offices across the African continent raises a number of key issues.[4]

Moreover, many other countries are studying the language as a 'foreign language.' However, English is the third language in some other countries like Tanzania, after mother tongues for every tribe, especially in rural areas, followed by Kiswahili which is the national language. In Tanzania, English is spoken by very few people (ca. 5% of the population), especially where non-Kiswahili speaking foreigners are involved, and during class sessions in secondary and higher education levels.[5]

English is learned for many different reasons. It may be an essential tool for education and business for some learners, the language of travel and related activities of sightseeing for others. English is required for social survival and employment for new immigrants in English-speaking countries. To some other people English is a popular language for the media, entertainment, the internet and other forms of electronic communication.

---

3. Alphonce, "The Language of Education," 140–141; Dachi, "Investing in Children's Right," 44.

4. Plonski, Teferrra and Brady, "Why are more African Countries,"1.

5. Mlay, "The Influence of the Language of Instruction," 48; Azaliwa, "The Impact of the Medium of Instruction," 391–392.

English as a Language of Teaching and Learning

In addition, for many other people, however, English is merely a language that they are obliged to study, but do not have any obvious need for it.[6]

Despite the emphasis on learning English in many parts of the world, it is worth remembering that most people can survive perfectly well in their own countries without ever having to use English. To these people, English is unnecessarily important. They do not require it to be a medium to understand something else. Moreover, Qorro's assertion is important when it comes to using English as a medium in order to understand something else. She writes that the reasons provided above for emphasizing on the use of English "are actually good reasons for *teaching English*, but not for *teaching in English*. Many have missed the point! *Teaching English* and *teaching in English* are two different things. While we all see the importance of *teaching English* as an international language and believe that it should be taught thoroughly as an additional language and as a school subject, some believe that the best way to *teach English* is to *teach in English*."[7] Qorro's assertion reminds us that the use of English as a language of instruction hardly does justice to students in secondary schools and higher education towards understanding the taught content and their participation in the creation of new knowledge. We will illustrate this point in the following review of literatures.

Furthermore, Kimizi states that the British initiated an English Language Teaching Support Project (ELTSP) in order to make sure that English remains as language of instruction in Tanzanian secondary schools and higher learning institutions, especially after the threat of eradication because of the rapid spread of Kiswahili. The project was well-funded with the opportunity for a considerable number of personnel investments for the sake of improving the teaching of English language in terms of developing curricular and syllabuses, providing some books and training the teachers to execute the prepared curricular and syllabuses.[8] However, Kimizi contends that, despite the high investments of the project in terms of finance and plans of execution, yet the Tanzanians' English language proficiency has still remained to the minimal level leaving the government in an

---

6. For more about the reasons of those who emphasize on English use in Tanzania please see the following Tanzanian Newspapers as listed by Qorro (2006:3-4): *Daily News* of March 5, 1999; *The Guardian* of April 5, 1999; *The Guardian* of April 13, 1999; *The Guardian* of February 16, 2000; *The Guardian* of February 19, 2000; and *The African* of August 7, 2003.

7. Qorro, "Does Language of Instruction affect Quality? 4.

8. Kimizi, "Why has the Language of Instruction? 12.

ambivalent situation in regard to the proper language of instruction to suit the current context.[9]

To us, the ELTSP indicates the English linguistic imperialism suggested by Robert Phillipson, whereby English language is made to dominate in former British colonized countries and the world as a whole in whatever possible means. It is possibly an endeavor at imposing "a single lens on the world."[10] It is a symbolic tool for power and authority of the former colonizers. In order to realize this power and authority in these former colonized African countries (colonized by Britain or any other European state), being proficient "in the [English language] is essential for upward social mobility and privileged positions in society."[11] As schools were used to alienate people from their native languages and cultural values in the USA, Australia and Wales, schools are used in a similar way to alienate African people from their native languages and cultural worldviews. In Tanzania and other Kiswahili speaking countries, Kiswahili seems to be a threat to this international hegemony of English as it is the Somali Language in Somalia.[12] However, as we will illustrate in the following subsections, despite its claim for hegemony in the world, English proves to be superficially enshrined in most multilingual world countries.

ENGLISH LANGUAGE AT A GLOBAL LEVEL

In this sub-section, we discuss the use of English as a teaching and learning medium at a global level and its shortcomings. Despite the ambivalence of the Tanzanian government about the issue of the language of instruction and the minimal proficiency of most people mentioned above, it is an undeniable fact that English strives to be the most widely used International language in the world. Telli emphasizes the statement made in the previous subsection about the resurgence of English thus: "English is now the first language of about 400 milions people in Britain, the United States and the Commonwealth, and it has become the dominant language of communication, business, aviation, entertainment, diplomacy and internet. . . . Today English is increasingly becoming the dominant global language whereby

---

9. Ibid.; cf. Mulokozi, "Baadhi ya Vipingamizi vya Kiutawala," 19; Kalmanlehto, "Mixed Domins," 26; Gawasike, "Lugha ya Kiswahili," 71.

10. Phillipson, *Linguistic Imperialism*, 189.

11. Ibid., 28.

12. Ibid., 27–28 .

English as a Language of Teaching and Learning

both the West and the East have become equally busy promoting it...."[13] Other languages include French, German, Portugal and Arabic. Therefore, this subsection concentrates on international parts apart from Africa.

In regard to the areas where English language dominates, Phillipson further notes:

> English has a dominant position in science, technology, medicine, and computers; in research, books, periodicals, and software; in transnational business, trade, shipping, and aviation; in diplomacy and international organizations; in mass media entertainment, news agencies, and journalism; in youth culture and sports; in education systems, as the most widely learnt foreign language.... [T]he spread of English is unique, both in terms of its geographical reach and as regards the depth of its penetration.[14]

Despite the international status of the English language stated by Telli and Phillipson above, yet it has some problems in terms of proficiency and academic performance of students in various countries which use it for teaching and learning. A study conducted by Manh in Vietnam on English language competency among students and lecturers showed that students and lecturers had generally low English proficiency.

In another investigation conducted from Danang University, which is one of the leading institutions in Vietnam, showed that 70% of the newly enrolled students had insufficient English proficiency to pursue studies in English. With such low English language competency, students were unable to comprehend lectures or materials in English. Considering lecturers, few of them had the proficiency to verbally communicate in English. Lecturers who earned academic qualifications abroad appeared to be good at English, although there were some concerns about their proficiency level, their ability to lecture at a level suitable for their students, and their interactions with students. If these concerns are not addressed, it may be difficult for students to learn from lecturers educated abroad.[15]

Following the findings of Manh, it is our opinion that if English proficiency is low among University lecturers and students, it leads to drawing a conclusion that the low proficiency has its roots in their language background at primary, secondary, and possibly at high schools. It is also our view that if the situation is bad among University communities, it will

---

13. Telli, "The Language of Instruction," 10.
14. Phillipson, *Linguistic Imperialism*, 6.
15. Manh, "English as a Medium of Instruction."

Looking Back

definitely be worse for lower levels of education. In addition, Manh's study seems to be very valid to the situation in Tanzania. English proficiency for most teachers at primary, secondary, and tertiary levels is extremely low. Some teachers try to avoid teaching in English because of low language proficiency; and hence, they lack confidence. This being the case, we are of the opinion that deliberate efforts should be employed in order to rectify the situation. Despite its importance and relevance, Manh's research is hereby challenged for not coming up with proposed solutions to the problems that he clearly indicated. This means that his study would be interesting if he indicated what was supposed to be done as solutions to the problems.

Al-Bakri, on the other hand, conducted research in Oman with a report entitled "Problematizing English Medium Instruction in Oman" whereby he came up with the views that many students liked to undertake their academic studies in Arabic language, which they were familiar with, rather than using English, which they had to learn and master it before knowing the contents in the subjects concerned. There was a controversial scenario in which some students interviewed liked English while others did not like it at all. Those who did not like it felt they were forced to study it without their consent.

In this research, it was further observed that some participants acknowledged the international status of English language and its important role in global communication, development, and employment. Others explained that "English [was] the language of money and business"[16] in the increasingly globalizing world. To these participants, the value of English was based on the contribution it had towards making international communication possible.

To our opinion, Al-Bakri's research conveys some exciting findings which are also valid and relevant to the existing situation in Tanzania. From the discussions that we hear in the Radio and televisions, there are some people who have the views that the country should declare Kiswahili as a medium of instruction at all levels while others reject this idea by giving the same points as those given by Al-Bakri's study in Oman. It is clearly understood that even countries which do not use English and other international languages as media of instruction still communicate with the rest of the world and value the cultures outside their own countries. Good examples here include Japanese, Chinese, and Russians. Telli reports thus about this: "most English textbooks and readings in China, from kindergarten

---

16. El Bakri, "Problematizing English Medium of Instruction," 7.

to university, either originated from the Anglo countries or represent Anglocentric culture in the name of authenticity. . . . As a result . . . many Chinese students know more the Anglo culture than the Chinese culture, and indeed, some young Chinese students seem to internalize the belief in the superiority of Anglo culture and the inferiority of their own culture."[17]

Furthermore, Wong in her study on the exposure of students to English in Hong Kong came up with the report titled "The Effectiveness of Using English as the Sole Medium of Instruction in English Classes."[18] It was determined in this report that students who strictly required to use English in class were more active in class participation. Exposure to English increased because students had no other options. However, if students were allowed to choose between English and Cantonese during lessons, they would naturally choose their native tongue.

In addition, it has now been proven that enforcement of a strict 'English-only policy' to students has a great positive impact on learning. A Class P students spoke English more frequently and freely in English classes because of strict "English-only policy" enforcement, while students in Class E generally chose to speak Cantonese among themselves (though not with their teacher); consequently this limited their English exposure, their practice, and quite obviously their confidence; and thus, their English proficiency grew less than that of Class P. This correlation clearly indicates how crucial the teacher's role is in creating a classroom language atmosphere that is conducive to learning.[19]

From this study, Wong found that students who were exposed to English and forced to use it throughout rather than using other languages increased their English proficiency compared to students from a school which had no emphasis on English. This is a very good finding which shows the importance of practice towards good performance. Undeniably, this is also the case in Tanzania, it looks like students who come from English Medium primary schools, when they join secondary schools, are far better in terms of English proficiency and performance because of great exposure to English. A study conducted by Komba and Bosco in the year 2015 in eight secondary schools at Mbeya region in Tanzania showed similar results. It indicated that students who joined secondary schools from English medium primary schools had better performance in their form one and

17. Telli, "The Language of Instruction," 12.
18. Wong, "The effectiveness of Using English."
19. Wong, "The effectiveness of Using English."

two examinations than those who came from ordinary Swahili medium primary schools. Their previous exposure to English language provided them with an opportunity to have the required vocabulary to understand what was taught and the questions asked.[20] This means that while students from ordinary primary schools struggle with vocabularies and sentence constructions, their fellows from English Medium primary schools are able to understand, and hence easily respond to questions asked by teachers in classrooms.

However, though insightful, Wong's and Komba and Bosco's studies do not discuss the fact that teachers' proficiency contributes to students' English proficiency. Their views are that students are supposed to be forced to speak English and be put in a situation where they will have no option other than speaking English, and that such forcing will help them improve their language. This cannot be denied. However, they should also consider the contribution of teachers in this aspect. If teachers are not English proficient, forcing students to speak English at the schools will most likely have less impact. Therefore, it is our opinion that the English proficiency has to start with teachers instead of just forcing students to adhere to the language which teachers themselves are not proficient.

In Tanzania, for instance, teachers at different levels of education do not have adequate English proficiency. Martha Qorro, in her survey on the use of English in Tanzanian schools, confirms this assertion when she reports: "Observation in some secondary school classrooms in Tanzania shows that most students and the majority of teachers in Tanzania are seriously handicapped when it comes to using English as a language of instruction: 'Only a handful of students take part in active learning and the majority of students simply sit and copy notes that their teachers have written on the blackboard.'"[21] Qorro, further adds, "If the teacher's handwriting is not legible students do not ask but simply copy words incorrectly since they are not able to distinguish correct from incorrect spelled words."[22] This problem trickles down to students in secondary level education, and when students go to the next level of education the problem continues because teachers have the same problem. Hence, the situation indicates that "In Tanzania secondary school classrooms and higher education the language

---

20. Komba & Bosco, "Do Students' Background in the Language?"
21. Qorro, "Does Language of Instruction?" 4; cf. Telli, "The Langauge of Instruction," 10.
22. Ibid.; cf. Telli, "The Language of Instruction," 10.

of instruction is not well understood by the majority of teachers and most students."[23]

Despite the coercion and the earlier exposure of students to English medium primary schools, there is an age factor to be considered. Gawi conducted a study on the age and time children begin studying English in Saudi Arabia. The title of his study was: "The Effects of Age Factor on Learning English: A Case Study of Learning English in Saudi Schools, Saudi Arabia." His aim was to examine the correlation between the age children start learning English and their proficiency in the language. Gawi discovered that pupils who started learning English at an early age, for instance from 5 to 6 years, became more competent in the language than those who started at a late age say from 12 years onwards. This is another useful study which came up with special ages for learning English and presumably any other languages. From Gawi's findings, it is worth noting that if we want our children to be English proficient, we have to make sure that they are exposed to the English language at their lower age as he proposed. For him, at this age, the children are inquisitive and able to learn quickly anything exposed to them, even those which some people consider being very hard for them.

Despite Gawi's good observation above, it is worth noting that his observation can never be valid and possible to all situations. Gawi did not manage to disclose this truth. In Tanzania, for instance, if you want your child to start learning English at the age of five years, that means you have to send the child to boarding English medium or International schools where they are good at English. However, sending the child to these schools, one must have enough money to pay for tuition fees, accommodation, and other charges. This means that boarding English medium international schools are for the few elites who can afford to pay for the owed amounts of money.[24]

In addition, many people in Tanzania hesitate to send their children to boarding schools at a tender age like this since at this age children are supposed to learn the culture and ethical values of their respective families and society. Sending them to boarding international schools means setting them aloof from the tutelage of parents, a thing which most people hardly do despite the financial constraints.

Despite the age factor, there are the questions of approach to teaching the language itself. Yao in his research done in 2010, with the title "A Study

23. Qorro, "Does Language of Instruction?" 4
24. Komba & John, "Investigation of Pupils' English Language," 56.

of the Teaching and Learning of English Grammar in the Chinese Junior Secondary School," examined the appropriate approach of teaching English grammar to junior secondary schools in China. The data gathered from the interviews, classroom observations, and questionnaires administered to teachers revealed several interesting findings on classroom phenomena. First, there were two main aspects which affected the use of inductive or deductive teaching approach to teach grammar. One is that the teaching approaches used in the textbook directly affected the teaching and learning approach. The textbook functioned as a guide to teachers, and they would follow the methods recommended in these textbooks. The other was the confidence and ability of teachers themselves to master English. Most Chinese teachers lacked proficiency in oral English and professional competency to use the inductive teaching method with students. That was why, a high number of teachers indicated that they consistently took additional training in teaching English as a foreign language. They usually took these classes by enrolling as part-time learners in teachers' colleges and regular universities. As a result of the training, more and more teachers came to realize the importance of learning via communication and situational learning in English teaching.

Second, exercises were a useful way to improve students' grammatical understandings. Students who did more exercises had better academic results in English language. Yao found in Shanghai that the advantage of exercises was to transfer grammar rules to various communicative topics and further into various situations or into compositions.

Third, it was also found that most learners rely on their teachers in oral English learning and could not learn it independently. There were more than 60% learners who agreed that the barriers of oral English learning were the negative transfers of mother language, difficulties in choosing the proper words, and oral English learning environment. Yao reached the two following conclusions; first, that there were more than 50% learners who had active attitudes to oral English learning. The results of the attitude in the survey showed that most learners were interested in oral English learning. And another conclusion was that most learners could not practice oral English independently and could not make their own learning plan but relied on their teachers. One barrier for oral English learning was lack of autonomy.

Fourth, a total of 94% learners agreed that the difference in thinking between China and West influenced their oral English learning to some extent.

In this aspect, 53% learners took the difference in thinking between China and West as the most difficult part in oral English learning. Therefore, following Yao's finding above, the greatest barrier to learners in China was how to overcome the difference of thinking between China and the West.

Fifth, that most students had difficulties in choosing the proper words and always made the same mistakes in choosing words. Vocabulary had been the barriers in oral English learning according to the percentage. Sixth, that 88% of learners agreed that the mother language influenced their oral English, and 75% of learners agreed that they always translated Chinese into English when they spoke in English. Hence, the mother language hindered the oral English learning in China.

Findings from Yao's research discussed above provide several factors which made the Chinese be unable to master English. In a nutshell, these factors include, teachers who themselves had no good command of English, students not making practice, influence of their mother languages, and the view of the Chinese towards English language and the Western culture. These factors are also valid to Tanzania because many pupils and students are taught English by teachers who are not competent in English; and hence, it becomes difficult for them to teach properly using it. Influence of the mother language is also another problem which Tanzanians share with people from China. Many Tanzanians think in their mother tongue, make a sentence in the mother tongue, translate it in Kiswahili, and then into English. This means that Tanzania also faces a similar problem of students not making enough practice in order to master the English language. It is always difficult to master the language without practicing it. There is a saying that "Practice Makes Perfect." Hence, if the Tanzanian government wants students to master the foreign language, deliberate efforts should be made to ensure that the factors mentioned above are overcome.

However insightful Yao's study is, yet it covered only a small sample of teachers and students in junior secondary schools, which is not an adequate representative of the huge population of China with over one billion people. In addition, this investigation was only conducted to schools in Shanghai city, which leaves us without knowledge of what happens to other cities in China. This means that findings from this metropolitan city cannot be generalized to the most rural areas of China. It should also be remembered that his study did not include private secondary schools.

ENGLISH LANGUAGE IN AFRICA

After surveying literatures in some parts of the world apart from Africa, this subsection concentrates on the use of English as a teaching and learning medium in African countries. Two examples from Southern Africa and Namibia will be used for this purpose. In the study with the title "English medium of instruction: a situation analysis" Uys et al conducted research in Southern Africa in the year 2007 to determine the reasons for the inability of teachers to assist their students to acquire academic literacy using English as a language of instruction. They reached the following reasons: First, teachers were often unaware of their inability to meet the language related requirements of their pupils. Second, teachers did not only lack the knowledge and skills for teaching the language skills, but also the insight to identify strategies that would promote effective learning. Third, teachers lacked the personal language proficiency required (both spoken and written) to assist their learners in the acquisition of academic literacy. Fourth, language proficiency was still regarded as the single most important prerequisite for effective learning. Teachers disregarded, or were ignorant of, the importance of applying methodological skills. Last, none of the teachers received training that could equip them with skills for effective teaching through the medium of English. However, the findings indicated the role of teachers in the process of learning and stressed the necessity for developing an appropriate training course to teachers for learning the subject content. Effective training in learning was seen as one of the most important factors in improving the level of academic literacy to South African learners. These are factors which really apply even to the rest of Africa and Tanzania in particular; there is no way we can help students learn and be successful without a positive role of teachers.

Another research was conducted by Nel and Muller published in the year 2010 with the title "The Impact of Teachers' limited English Proficiency on English Second Language Learners in South African Schools." Its aim was to determine the English language proficiency of teachers in South African schools. The researchers found that teachers made basic errors such as grammatical errors, incorrect use of tenses and spelling errors. This was found to be generally applicable to almost all teachers. Nevertheless, this study was based on teachers in South Africa, and was found that students were taught by incompetent teachers.

This study revealed very useful findings. It was obvious for students who were taught by incompetent teachers to be poor both in English and in other subjects which were taught in English. The study from South Africa, though could hardly be an adequate representation of all African countries, highlighted that Africa, and Tanzania in particular, should have a close eye on the competency of teachers both at primary and secondary school levels because they have direct impact on students' academic performance. It is factual that incompetent teachers are likely to produce incompetent students.

Another study was conducted by Chavez in the year 2016 in Namibia with the title "Rights in Education and Self-Identity: Education and Language of Instruction in Namibia." The study focused on the effectiveness of using a language not fully understood by students towards grasping the taught content. Chavez conducted an investigative examination at a school in Windhoek, the capital of Namibia, and revealed that "22.4% of students in Grade 8 were not functionally literate in English, and that 49.2% of the students had numeracy skills below a Grade 7 level. All of the students that tested below the required level came from primary schools where English was used as the language of instruction from Grade 1 rather than a mother tongue. Additionally, many educators in Namibia complained that students depended on thoughtless memorization of subject matter, which they merely repeat back on examinations without fully understanding. . . ."[25] The above findings of the study showed that the goals of intrinsic education could not be accomplished when students were instructed in a language that they did not fully understand.

Research has shown that there was a strong and positive correlation between literacy in the native language and learning English, and that the degree of children's native language proficiency is a strong predictor of their English language development. This means that in order for education to help students in Namibia develop their capabilities, it should be presented through a language medium that students fully understand, and through which they can competently and confidently express themselves. When children are literate in their mother tongue, they are able to establish a set of skills that will then be transferred over when they learn a new language.

The situation in Namibia is not so much different from the situation in Tanzania and in most other African countries. Pupils and students in most African countries are fluent in local or national languages; and when, unfortunately, they are taught in a language which they are seriously struggling with it, it becomes very difficult for them to understand. For example, Kiswahili is widely used and known for a big population in Tanzania. If

---

25. Chavez, "Rights in Education," 193.

Tanzania taught pupils and students in this language, it would be easy for them to comprehend and respond positively.

ENGLISH LANGUAGE IN TANZANIA

After discussing some literatures which highlight the use of English in secondary schools in Africa, this section focuses on Tanzania, the study area. As highlighted in the introduction of this book, Tanzania is a multilingual society with over 120 native local languages spoken in the country.[26] English is essential, as it is the language which links Tanzania with the rest of the world through technology, commerce and administration. However, it is the learning of Kiswahili that enables Tanzania's students to keep in touch with their cultural values and heritage and build their African identity as they grow up, not English or any other foreign language.

In Tanzania, English is taught as a compulsory subject in most schools at pre-primary and primary education levels, whereas at post-primary education it is the compulsory medium of instruction. With regard to Kiswahili, it is the medium of instruction for the majority pre-primary and primary schools while at secondary education level it is taught as a compulsory subject and as an option subject at tertiary education. This way of using both English and Kiswahili in education demonstrates the ambivalence in the LoI in the country.

In their study with the title "Investigation of Pupils' English Language Abilities in Tanzania," done in 2015, Komba and John examined the effectiveness of English language as a medium of instruction in English medium primary schools in Tanzania. They envisaged that after the seven years of learning English language as well as using the same as the medium of instruction, the English medium primary school pupils would be able to perform better in the specified abilities. However, the findings of this study revealed that the majority of pupils could not perform well in the tested abilities. Unfortunately, they concluded that pupils were not very good in terms of English writing, reading, understanding and speaking despite their use of this language as the LoI. In Tanzania, it is considered

26. There is not a consensus yet among scholars in regard to the exact number of vernacular languages spoken by Tanzanian ethnic groups. Some scholars list 120 languages, others 129, others 128, while the survey of the Languages of Tanzania Project of 2009 lists 164 languages (see Wamalwa, Adika & Kevogo, "Multilingualism and Language Attitudes," 53, Petzell, "The Linguistic Situation in Tanzania," 136, and Sa, "Language Policy for Education," 1).

English as a Language of Teaching and Learning

that pupils from English Medium primary schools could be good at English as compared to pupils from ordinary schools which use Kiswahili as a language of instruction; and parents are motivated to admit their children to such schools because of this anticipation. Therefore, the findings by Komba and John indicate that Tanzania still has a long way to go in order to really help children improve their English language proficiency even in English medium primary schools.

However, Komba and John conducted research in English medium schools where students' parents have enough money to support them. Not every parent in Tanzania can send his or her children in English medium schools. This is fairly obvious in Tanzania where the best schools like Feza Boys and Girls, Mariana Boys and Girls, Kaizirege, and others are too expensive to normal parents to afford. In these schools, students pay over six million Tanzania shillings per annum. The schools have become special for children from the well-to-do families. In addition, children who join or survive in these schools are the highly intelligent ones. Most of them who are not gifted are screened out in the process before they reach Standard Seven. The intention for these schools is to have a few students who will perform nicely and hence maintain their reputation. Therefore, though Komba and John's study is insightful, it could add more value if it were a comparative study trying to compare the effectiveness of English and Kiswahili as languages of instruction in primary schools. The comparison could justify its importance as a language of instruction over Kiswahili which is spoken by most people, even in the homes.

However, a comparative study was conducted by Yoradi in the year 2013 in four secondary schools within Mvomero District. Yoradi taught Biology subject to students in English and then in Kiswahili and provided them tests in Kiswahili and in English. Yoradi's study found that students had better performance when Kiswahili was used than when English was used as a language of instruction. This indicated that students understood better the subject matter when Kiswahili was used as a language of instruction than when English was used.

Despite the comparison of the two languages done by Yoradi, Mtallo also conducted research in the year 2015 to compare and contrast the situation in teaching and learning English in the two countries of Vietnam and Tanzania. The study presented Phan Le Ha's major observations in the way English language was learnt and taught in Vietnam and compared this situation with the Tanzanian context. Mtallo found that although the language policy dictated the use of English language as the medium of instruction, its practice was not yet successful.

In Tanzanian classrooms, for instance, teachers tended to code-switch and code-mix between English and Kiswahili in order to help learners understand their subject contents better. This practice demonstrated vividly the mismatch between language policy and classroom practice in Tanzania. Despite the fact that the use of English language seems to have economic and social merits to developing countries like Tanzania as motivated by the overwhelming globalization, the language has most likely not yet managed to lift up these countries to the intended level of development. Therefore, there is a necessity for Tanzania, as one of the developing countries, to think on how it can revisit its language policy so that it reflects the requirements and interests of Tanzanians. The revisit is necessary because the existing policy seems to be a blessing theoretically, but a curse practically as evidenced by some classroom practices presented in Mtallo's study discussed above.

What is code switching and code mixing as far as class instruction is concerned? The concept of "code switching" relates to the concept of "code mixing." The two concepts are, in most cases, interchangeable. Line Kjolstad Gran, taking ideas from Saville-Troike, defines the concepts of "code-switching" and "code mixing" thus: "code-switching refers to a change in languages within a single speech event. Code-switching is understood as an intersentential change, meaning that the switch in languages takes place between sentences. Code-mixing on the other hand refers to an intrasentential change, which implies that the language switch takes place within the same sentence...."[27]

Furthermore, Vuzo adds, "Code mixing is seen as the unsystematic result of not knowing very well one of the languages involved and is a form of linguistic decay.... On the contrary, code switching does not necessarily indicate a deficiency on the part of the speaker but may result from complex bilingual skills of the speaker."[28] In brief, the difference between the two terminologies is that one action (code mixing) is done when the teacher is not knowledgeable of the language used in teaching, while the other action (code switching) is done when the teacher is fully conversant with the language of teaching and the action is done as a strategy to enhance

---

27. Gran, "Language of Instruction," 20; cf. Brock-Utne, "English as the Langauge of Instruction?" 3–11; Modupeola, "Code-Switching as Teaching Strategy," 92–93; Mlay, "The Influence of the Language of Instruction," 14–15 and 27–28; Dzahene-Quarshie, "Language Policy," 33–34.

28. Vuzo, "Stakeholders' Opinions," 129–130.

more clarity of the taught content.[29] However, Kadeghe calls the language which emerges from the interactions of code switching and code mixing as "*trans-lingualism.*"[30]

Trans-lingualism, according to Kadeghe is what makes some students acquire higher grades in examinations. In the case of Tanzanian secondary schools, trans-lingualism is neither English nor Kiswahili. Rather, it is "*Kiswanglish,*" the language that emerges as the teacher code-switches and code-mixes the two languages.[31] Hence, code switching and code mixing are tools or mechanisms, each serving its own purpose. Code mixing is the tool for teachers to hide their weakness or incompetence on the language of instruction, while code-switching is a tool for the teacher to play two roles: to be "curriculum implementer" (when using English, the language of the curriculum which is not clearly understood by learners) and "students' facilitator" enabling them to comprehend the taught content using the language they are able to understand clearly.[32]

In concluding this part, we may say that, from what Mtallo highlighted in his study above, it is obvious that most Tanzanian students have negative feelings on the use of English as a medium of instruction for various reasons. First, the use of English language seems to torture students' minds unnecessarily, without enjoying to use the language, just forcing them to use it in a slavery way. It is evident that most of them are not comfortable with it at all.

Second, learning English in such a hostile environment becomes a painful experience for learners, and may end up creating negative attitudes towards the language and the subject content studied. Third, the "*Speak English Only,*" "or "*No English No Service*" rule which enforces students to communicate in English degrades African languages, like Kiswahili their national language, and creates in the young minds of learners the impression that English is the only legitimate language for producing and disseminating knowledge, a thing which is hardly true.[33] Moreover, teachers themselves, because of their low proficiency in both spoken and written English, are the first ones to break such a rule. The teachers' inability to adhere to the rule which they themselves have set is a clear indication

29. Ibid.
30. Kadeghe, "Code-Switching in Tanzanian Classrooms," 118.
31. See Ibid., 119–122 for examples.
32. Ibid., 124, cf. Bwenge, "Code-Switching," and Bwenge, *The Tongue between*, for the code switching of languages in the Tanzanian Parliamentary discourse.
33. Qorro, Does Language of Instruction Affect Quality?" 9.

that English remains foreign and inappropriate to ensure well understood content of what is learned in both written and spoken English.

Where then is the source of the problem of improper use of English language for teaching and learning in Tanzania? Yohana P. Msanjila reports that the problem of lack of proper English language proficiency in Tanzanian secondary and higher education students and teachers does not primarily belong to individual students and teachers. Rather, it is systemic. It is of the government's educational system as a whole. In his words, Msanjila says: "*Tafiti zilizofanywa na wanataaluma mbalimbali . . . zinaonyesha kwamba tatizo linalosababisha wanafunzi wengi washindwe kuzungumza au kuandika Kiingereza vizuri katika masomo yao siyo wanafunzi wenyewe bali ni mfumo mzima wa elimu ambao kimsingi unahitaji kufanyiwa tathmini ili uboreshwe.*" [Literal Translation: Researches done by various scholars . . . indicate that the problem causing most students become unable to speak or write English well in their studies does not emanate from individual students; rather, it is of the whole educational system which principally requires evaluation for the sake of improvement.][34] Msanjila proposes that improvement should be done on the way teachers training is done, the availability of teaching facilities in schools, the availability of text and reference books, and the way questions for testing students are prepared. For him, punishing students who speak Kiswahili as a way of enforcing them to learn English is unfair and going against human rights because it is not their mistake but of their government and its educational plans.[35]

The difficulty for students to understand the taught content caused by the language of instruction barrier stated above was confessed by students in the research conducted by Ndalichako and Komba in the year 2014 in some community secondary schools in Tanzania. In a focused group discussion, one student had the following response in one of the researchers' surveyed schools:

> The biggest challenge here at our school is mainly English language. Our English language proficiency is very low and teachers are not doing anything to help us! Teachers have not implemented the English speaking policy which requires students to speak English. They use Kiswahili in teaching but students cannot use Kiswahili in responding to the national examination questions. We are all required

---

34. Msanjila, "Hali ya Kiswahili katika Shule za Sekondari," 213; cf. Qorro, "Does Language of Instruction affect Quality?" 4

35. Ibid., 213, 216.

> to write in English. So at the end of the day students know points for a particular question but the problem is how to write them in examination paper in proper English language. . . .[36]

Hence, from students as one of the main stakeholders, English is confirmed to be less effective towards students' acquisition of proper taught content and proper students' use to answer questions in examinations.

In their study done in 2013 in Dodoma Tanzania with the title "Students' Perceived Level of English Proficiency in Secondary Schools in Dodoma, Tanzania," Makewa, Role, and Tuguta further focused on the perception of students in Dodoma region in Tanzania towards English as a language of teaching and learning. Makewa, Role and Tuguta found the following; first, the overall mean perceived level of proficiency was on average. This level of proficiency indicated that respondents had some problems with spoken English. They doubted their speaking skills. It was further found that the problem experienced in second language learning related to the fact that students attempted to learn another language while having their own prestigious language, which led them to putting less emphasis on the new language in order to master it. Following this investigation, Kiswahili language blocks mastery of English because it is not only the most widespread language but also the most prestigious and dominant language in both written and spoken communications. Teachers and students speak it almost all the time in all places and to all people where they live.

Second, the study by Makewa, Role and Tuguta also discovered that most students had moderate level of English language anxiety. It was obvious that students tended to be self-conscious about speaking English in public or to a stranger. Some learners of English were intimidated when they conversed with a better speaker of English. The little English they knew tended to disappear. The whole of this situation was mostly caused by anxiety.

This study by Makewa, though is limited to secondary schools of only one region of Tanzania, with a negligible representation of secondary schools in rural areas, unveils the real situation of most people in Tanzania. This situation is what Mligo faced during his study abroad as described in the beginning of the previous chapter. Excessive use of Kiswahili hampers the development of English. In many offices, schools, and even where it is

---

36. Ndalichako & Komba, "Students' Subject Choice," 54; cf. Mlay, "The Influence of the Language of Instruction," 16; Mwinsheikhe, "Using Kiswahili as a Medium of Instruction."

written "no English no service," Kiswahili is still prominent. In addition, most Tanzanians are not confident enough when speaking English with people they feel are better than them. They develop unnecessary anxiety and fear. One can dare to say that, there is a necessity to pay a close attention to what could be the solutions to this problem of lack of adequate English proficiency and confidence in this economically and technologically pressing era of globalization.

TEACHING AND LEARNING USING OTHER LANGUAGES

The world has several countries which do not use English as their language of instruction and not their first language. Some of such countries include China, Japan, Russia, North Korea, and India just to mention a few of them. These countries are far ahead of most developing countries, like Tanzania, in terms of development. Indeed, these countries are not even using their colonial master's languages like French, Portugal and Germany. Therefore, we agree with Gawasike when he writes:

> *Licha ya ukweli ulio dhahiri kuwa Tanzania imeweza kujenga na kukuza umoja wa kitaifa kutokana na matumizi ya lugha ya Kiswahili, bado kuna hisia kwamba kutumia Kiswahili kutaifanya nchi ya Tanzania kutokuwa na maendeleo ya kisayansi na kiteknolojia miongoni mwa baadhi ya watu, hasa wanasiasa na wasomi. Hata hivyo, inafaa ikumbukwe kuwa hakuna nchi yoyote duniani ambayo imekuwa na maendeleo ya kuridhisha ya kisayansi na kiteknolojia bila ya kutumia lugha yake ya taifa katika mawasiliano ya nyanja zote ikiwa ni pamoja na kutolea elimu.*[37]
>
> [Literal translation: Despite the fact that Tanzania has managed to build a national unity by the use of Kiswahili, yet there are feelings among people that using Kiswahili will make the Tanzanian country deprived of scientific and technological development, especially among the learned. However, it is important to remember that there is no any country in the world which has achieved adequate scientific and technological development without using its national language in communication to all sectors including teaching.]

To our opinion, though it is probably true that English is the first spoken International language in the world it looks like developing countries have

---

37. Gawasike, "Lugha ya Kiswahili," 74.

unnecessarily put so much emphasis on English as if without it there can be no development. It is unfortunate that in these countries, in most cases, a person is considered to be more educated if that person speaks English well. In these countries, therefore, English is adored and magnified more than the native languages which are fluently spoken and understood by the majority.

In fact, Tanzanians have to ask and re-ask themselves why they should not make special emphasis on Kiswahili and promote it to be a teaching and learning language at all levels of their educational system as many researchers have just claimed in their researches. To our opinion, it seems that policy-makers hesitate to decide on this new move because of various unscientific reasons leaving the country undecided on which language should be emphasized as the language of instruction, especially in primary schools in Tanzania.

THE EMERGING GAP OF KNOWLEDGE

The question of the language of instruction in educational systems posses a great challenge to various nations in the world. As we have seen in this chapter, many people from different parts of the world, including Tanzania, have greatly done research on the use of English as a teaching and learning medium. However, no study among those surveyed in this chapter has been conducted extensively on the use of English and performance of students in community secondary schools in Tanzania, and particularly in Mbeya District Council, the area selected to represent the other districts in Tanzania. This is the gap which this study intends to fill. Since such schools are numerous and prevalent in the Tanzanian context, almost in each ward, we found it important to study extensively on the use of English language in these schools because the schools experience poor performance problems more than any other types of schools in the Tanzanian educational system.

CONCLUSION

Generally, this chapter has examined several journal articles and books in order to determine the way researchers say about the use of English as a language of instruction. In a funnel-like form (from the general to specific) we have staged the review starting with the general world, Africa and Tanzania as our main focus. Different scholars from different parts of the world view the use of English as being a stumbling block to teaching and learning in their countries. They view it in this way because of its interference with the cultural orientation of people in those countries and its ability to create inequalities among people, and make them incompetent in the employment market within those countries. Therefore, the chapter forms the necessary foundation and context to deal with the research on the use of English in community secondary schools in Tanzania focusing on Mbeya Region.

Chapter 3

Laying Out the Way
Hypothesis and Methodology

"If the most distinctive feature of science is its empirical nature, the next most important characteristic is its set of procedures which show not only how findings have been arrived at, but are sufficiently clear to fellow-scientists to repeat them, i.e. to check them out with the same or other materials and thereby test the results."

—Cohen & Manion, Perspectives on Classrooms, 12.

INTRODUCTION

Having reviewed the relevant literatures and determined the possible gap of knowledge, this chapter lays down the method or procedure used in research. The word "method" here means "a way' or "a means" of doing something. Mligo defines the term method thus: "In the research report context, the 'method' is the whole means through which you investigated the problem to reach to the conclusions you have reached. Here the 'method' concept does not only comprise the techniques or tools for data collection.... it is similar to the methodological perspective...."[1] Hence, this chapter discusses the research method; it discusses the various procedures employed in the research process to yield the evidence for making its point. It describes the process which was used in the field from preparation

---

1. Mligo, *Introduction to Research*, 113, cf. Jonker & Pennink, *The Essence of Research*, 21–22; Cohen, Manion & Morrison, *Research Methods in Education*, 165.

stage for data collection, data analysis to presentation of findings or reporting. We also describe the hypothesis which was an intelligent guess of what was expected to be the result of the study findings.

The chapter is divided into the following parts: the hypothesis, the research design, the present area of study, and the sources of data, both primary and secondary sources of data. Moreover, the chapter describes the population and sample size whereas, the sampling design, the data collection methods or instruments and the data presentation and analysis procedures. By laying the above listed procedures, the chapter argues that a *mixed method* type of approach is more convenient in investigating the impact of using English as a language of teaching and learning to students' academic performance in developing countries like Tanzania.

HYPOTHESIS AND DESIGN

There are several definitions of the concept of hypothesis proposed by scholars of research. However, Koul defines a hypothesis as "a tentative or working proposition suggested as a solution to a problem."[2] Koul also views the term hypothesis epistemologically as being made up of two words *"hypo"* meaning less than, and a *"thesis"* which means a proposition. Following this definition, the hypothesis comes from the thesis. It is less than the actual proposition. This view is supported by Mligo when he writes: "the thesis is wider than the hypothesis in the manner that it might not be tested empirically, but must be argued for or against. This means that all hypotheses are potentially theses but not all theses are potentially hypotheses."[3] In our view, from Koul and Mligo's definitions above, the researcher should have a guessed answer to the problems facing the community or society. The guessed answer, which is called a hypothesis, should be tested its validity through its variables. Moreover, according to Ary, Jacobs and Sorensen, a "hypothesis is a statement describing relationships among variables that is tentatively assumed to be true."[4] In this definition, Ary, Jacobs & Sorensen view testing of the hypothesis through the variables it contains as being the central element for the researcher to attain new knowledge because the hypothesis is just assumed to be true.

2. Koul, *Methodology of Educational Research*, 72.
3. Mligo, *Introduction to Research*, 34.
4. Ary, Jacobs & Sorensen, *Introduction to Research in Education*, 7.

Following the above definitions, we can summarize that a hypothesis is an intelligent guess. It is an expected result that the researcher intends to obtain and has to be proved wrong or right by the collection of relevant data. The testing of this hypothesis is done by testing the variables in it; and it is mostly done in empirical quantitative researches. Hence, through testing the variables in quantitative researches the researcher tests both the validity of the hypothesis and the theory where the hypothesis originates.

The study for this book was mainly quantitatively designed to test variables (though supplemented by some qualitative data) and was guided by a hypothesis that *the low proficiency of English of students and teachers who teach them causes poor performance in Form Four summative examinations in community secondary schools in Tanzania*. It means that the study was conducted to prove or disapprove this hypothesis after the collection of data in relation to poor academic performance of students (dependent variable) and the low English proficiency of teachers and students (independent variable), interpreting and analyzing them. We conducted research with the convictions that if the above hypothesis was proved right, we would have all the confidence to clearly tell the academic community and other educational stakeholders that it was the low English proficiency which led to poor performance in Tanzanian community secondary schools. If the hypothesis was wrong, we would recommend that there was a necessity to conduct another study to determine the factors for the poor academic performance in the schools in question.

The hypothesis plays a great role in the consolidation of the design for the study because it clearly indicates that a quantitative research is required. On the one hand Bogdan & Biklen define research design to be referring "to the researchers' plan of how to proceed."[5] It is the arrangement of conditions for the collection and analysis of data in a manner that aims to combine relevance to the research purpose with economy in procedure. Kombo and Tromp, on the other hand, define research design as "the glue that holds all the elements in a research project together."[6] However, Mligo states that research design answers four important questions: first, "what approach will you use in your research and why." Second, "within what theoretical [or philosophical] framework' do you position your research?" Third, "from whom will data be collected and how," and fourth, "which

---

5. Bogdan & Biklen, *Qualitative Research for Education*, 49.
6. Kombo and Tromp, *Proposal and Thesis Writing*, 71.

ethical issues will you take into account in collecting research data?"[7] In answering the four questions, research design can be thought of as being the master plan of a research that throws light on how the study is to be conducted. Research design is similar to an architectural framework which shows what starts, what follows, and what ends.

In the study for this book, we used a *mixed methods research design* which uses both quantitative and qualitative approaches.[8] The quantitative approach to research uses numbers (statistics) in presenting and analyzing data. It is located within the positivist paradigm of research whereby the researcher has to be detached from the informants (objects) who provide the required data. Positivism is the belief that observational data produces human knowledge as the data undergo scientific interpretation. This philosophical thought started in Ancient Greek and has been an ongoing theme in the history of Western thought to the present day. Corbetta asserts that the Western positivist thought was clearly consolidated in the early 19th century by the French philosopher and founding sociologist Auguste Comte (1798—1857). In the positivist paradigm, according to Corbetta, knowledge is objective and obtained through the use of rigorous scientific procedures.[9]

The collection of quantitative data in this paradigm is through the use of standardized instruments, such as structured questionnaires. In this book, we selected to use quantitative approach in the positivist paradigm because we were interested to get some statistical research information which one could not obtain by using qualitative methods. This means that quantitative approach was the main approach selected and qualitative approach was supplementary. The qualitative approach was mainly used when interviewing District education officials at the area of our study and discussing the presented themes using the existing literatures.[10]

As the quantitative approach belongs to positivism, qualitative approach belongs to the interpretivist paradigm (philosophical thought) which has several other branches. However, the main emphasis of this paradigm is the interpretation of existing social realities as participants in those realities experience them. In sociology, interactionism, one of the branches of

---

7. Mligo, *Introduction to Research*, 49.

8. See Bryman, *Quantity and Quality in Social Research*, 126–154.

9. Corbetta, *Social Research*, 13–17, cf. Cohen, Manion & Morrison, *Research Methods*, 9–19.

10. Ibid., cf. Lund, "The Qualitative-Quantitative Distinction," 18–20.

the interpretivist paradigm, is a theoretical perspective in which society is thought to be a product of the everyday social interactions among people. Therefore, the interpretation of reality in the interactionist perspective depends on the way individuals experience it in their real life situations.[11]

According to Corbetta, the German historian, psychologist, and hermeneutics philosopher Wilhelm Dilthey (1833—1911) is considered to be the founder of the interpretivist paradigm when reacting to Comte's positivism. He was supported by other scholars like George Herbert Mead, Max Weber, and Herbert Blumer who also made several contributions to the intepretivist theory, especially in the branch of interactionism. Interactionism, as a branch of interpretivist paradigm, focuses on the way human beings act, or make conscious choices regarding their behavior that proceed from how they interpret situations. In other words, human beings are not simply reacting to social stimuli; they are also social actors and must adjust their behavior based on the actions of other social actors.[12] It is through this interaction where the interpretation emerges.

Strictly speaking, interactionism examines how different social actors make sense of or interpret the behavior of those around them. This information can be used to understand the social construction of the world, which is focused on not only the meanings that they give to behavior, but also on how they interpret the meanings of behavior from fellow people around them. Under interactionism, reality or knowledge is subjective, and informants who provide research information are subjects. As said earlier, in this study, we also used the interactionist perspective, within interpretivism, which involves the use of qualitative methods of data collection such as observations, interviews and document reviews because of our interest in the interaction between teachers and students inside and outside the classrooms in community secondary schools and how they make sense of each other in their interactions (i.e., how students view at their teachers and how teachers view their students in terms of the use of English language and academic performance).

Why use mixed methods design in this study? Creswell defines a mixed methods research design as "a procedure for collecting, analyzing and mixing both quantitative and qualitative methods in a single study or a series of studies to understand a research problem."[13] We employed this

11. Ibid., 20–25 and 33–36.
12. Ibid., 20–25.
13. Creswell, *Educational Research*, 535.

research design because there were both qualitative and quantitative data to be collected and analyzed which enhanced a better understanding of the problem. Qualitative approach helped to examine the interactions between students and teachers in the use of English and the interpretations of experiences which emerged from this interaction; while quantitative approach, as the main approach used in the study, provided the statistical information from informants' participation in the learning process, their responses to asked questions, and the statistics of their performance in the course of using English language as a medium of instruction.

AREA OF STUDY AND SOURCES OF DATA

Having justified the use of a mixed methods research design and what it entails, this section responds to the question: from whom were the data collected? It briefly discusses about the place where the study was conducted while the detailed description of it will be done in the next chapter. It should be born in mind that, since Tanzania is a large country, it is hardly possible to conduct a detailed and focused research within the whole country without being superficial. In order to focus our study and avoid superficiality, this study was conducted in Mbeya District Council, formerly known as Mbeya Rural District, and in a few selected Wards. The selected Wards are Inyala where we visited Imezu secondary school, Ijombe Ward where we visited two schools: Nsongwi Juu and Iwalanje secondary schools. The last Ward is Utengule Usongwe where we visited Usongwe secondary school. We had some reasons for selecting Mbeya District Council as a representative of community secondary schools in Tanzania. First, students' performance at both primary and secondary school levels was extremely low in Mbeya District Council. The low performance experienced in these schools is still the reality to most community secondary schools within the country. Second, there were no tuition centers in Mbeya District Council as it was the case for Mbeya City and other Districts within Tanzanian regions. Tuition centers can help to improve students' performance in English, and in other subjects. Since most community secondary schools in Tanzania are located at Ward levels within districts, they are hardly located in urban places. This makes tuitions mostly unavailable. Third, there were not many English medium primary schools in this area of research; and on top of that, very few people could afford sending their pupils to such schools because of economic hardships in the area. As it is in this study area, people in most areas in Tanzania where community secondary schools are located have poor economic statuses. It is this poor area of Mbeya District Council where data were collected for this book, and where sources for data collection were drawn, to represent the locations of the majority community secondary schools in the other regions and districts of Tanzania.

What are data, and what type of sources were employed for this study? On the one hand, Bogdan & Biklen define the term data as "rough materials researchers collect from the world they are studying; they are the particulars that form the basis of analysis."[14] Data include materials the people actively record when doing the study. Data also include what others have created and the researcher finds such as diaries, photographs, official documents and newspaper articles. On the other hand, Mligo distinguishes between "research information" and "research data." According to him, research information are unorganized raw materials just collected from the study area, while research data are materials collected from the study area and organized for analysis to yield research evidence in order to support a particular claim. [15] However, in this book, the concepts of research information and research data are used interchangeably.

Moreover, in this study, we used two major sources of data; namely, primary and secondary sources of data. We used both primary and secondary sources of data because there are information which were to be collected from the field directly while other information already existed in the Mbeya District Council's Education Office. Such information included the number of students at sampled schools, students' performance records of previous years which could be found in the District Education Office, Ward Education Coordinator's (WEC) Offices and in the Head Teachers' Offices. Let us briefly consider the concepts of primary and secondary sources of data.

Primary Sources

On the one hand, Kombo and Tromp define primary data as "information gathered directly from respondents."[16] On the other hand, Mligo defines primary data as the "raw materials that are not used anywhere else. These are data that you collect for the first time from the source. . . . "[17] The sources where

---

14. Bogdan & Biklen, *Qualitative Research for Education*, 106.
15. Mligo, *Introduction to Research*, 92–93.
16. Kombo and Tromp, *Proposal and Thesis Writing*, 100.
17. Mligo, *Introduction to Research*, 94.

primary data are collected are called primary sources where; these are places where one collects first hand data. Mligo, quoting from Gall, Borg and Gall, defines a primary source as "a document (e.g., journal article, or dissertation) that was written by individuals who actually conducted the research study or who formulated the theory or opinions that are described in the document."[18] The primary data are usually collected from sources through questionnaires, interviews, Focus Group Discussions (FGDs), observation and experimental studies. However, in this study, we collected original data from the field using two major research instruments, which are questionnaires and interviews. We used these two instruments because they fitted adequately to the mixed research method used. Quantitative data were collected through questionnaires, and qualitative data were collected through interviews.

Secondary Sources

Kombo and Tromp define secondary data as information "neither collected directly by the user nor specifically for the user."[19] It involves gathering data that has been collected by someone else. Mligo's definition resembles that of Kombo and Tromp. Mligo writes: "Secondary data are raw materials that you use for the second, third, or more times. These are data that were collected and used by someone else, and you decide to use them in your research. For example, data from books, from journal articles, from newspapers, from conference papers, and from magazines."[20] Therefore, Mligo quoting Gall, Borg and Gall, defines a secondary source as "a document written by someone who did not actually do the research, develop the theories, or express the opinions that they have synthesized into the literature review . . ."[21] In this study, we reviewed different published and unpublished materials to advance the discussion of data. The study also sought information from the Mbeya District Councils' Office, Ward Coordinators, and from Heads of schools in order to prove or disprove the stated hypothesis. Therefore, secondary data were very useful in various stages of this study, especially the literatures review and data presentations, analysis and discussion chapters.

---

18. Ibid., 119.
19. Kombo and Tromp, *Qualitative Research in Education*, 100.
20. Mligo, *Introduction to Research*, 95.
21. Mligo, *Doing effective Fieldwork*, 119.

POPULATION AND SAMPLE

After discussing the primary and secondary data and their sources, this section turns to the population and samples of data collection for this book. Kombo and Tromp see population as a "group of individuals, objects or items from which samples are taken for measurement (for example a population of students)."[22] Population is an entire group of persons or elements that have at least one thing in common, for instance, students at a particular school or university, people in a certain ethnic group, soldiers, whores, homosexuals, heterosexuals, teachers, and doctors. Since each of the mentioned groups comprises of many representatives, a sample of few of them within a particular group is selected and studied to represent the other people within that group. Following this understanding, the samples for this study were drawn from four distinct populations of students, teachers, community members, and officials at the district office. The samples taken comprised of all eligible individuals from the age of 12 and above. The samples involved students, teachers, community members, and Officials at the District Office. A total of 110 respondents were involved from the mentioned populations.

The question here is what it means by sampling and how sampling was done to have the required samples. On the one hand, Kothari defines sampling as "the selection of some part of an aggregate or totality on the basis of which a judgment or inference about the aggregate or totality is made."[23] Alreck & Settle, on the other hand, define sampling design that it "simply means taking part of some population to represent the whole population."[24] Following these definitions, sampling techniques can be classified into two main types: probability or random sampling, and non-probability or non-random sampling. In the probability or random sampling, every member has a chance to be included in the sample, whereas the non-probability or non-random sampling does not provide an equal chance for each member to be included in the sample because the researcher intentionally selects the sample to fulfill a particular purpose.

Following the above understanding, to a larger extent, this study employed random sampling techniques to classes and students within the class. It also used the same technique to teachers within the selected schools. This sampling design was used in order to provide equal chances

---

22. Kombo and Tromp, *Proposal and Thesis Writing*, 77.
23. Kothari, *Research Methodology*, 152.
24. Alreck & Settle, *The Survey Research*, 54.

to students and teachers to provide information for the use of English at their respective schools. However, at a District level, the study used a no-probability sampling. Convenience sampling was employed to conduct interviews with District Education Officers. This was used because it required specific people with specific information in regard to the use of English at their respective Wards. Moreover, the officials themselves were specific people; there was no room for choice.

INSTRUMENTS FOR DATA COLLECTION

After selecting the sample using an appropriate sampling design, what followed was the collection of data, the information for research purposes. Data collection is vital as it stimulates new ideas, promotes decision making, and clarifies facts. The study employed three methods of questionnaires, interviews, and documentary analysis for collecting both primary and secondary data.[25] We developed both open and close-ended questionnaires which were provided to different respondents in the selected samples. Close-ended questionnaires were crucial for respondents to choose the correct answers from the list set by the researcher whereas open-ended questionnaires required respondents to provide their own views or opinions about an issue based on the question asked.

Moreover, the study also collected information through conducting interviews with some students in the selected community secondary schools in the study area as well as District Officials. We ensured that a good rapport was established which fostered obtaining more information from participants. Interview, as a method for obtaining empirical data, was very useful because it enabled us to probe the participants in the course of the interview sessions and follow them up after the research was done in order to acquire more information about the issues at hand.

DATA ANALYSIS AND PRESENTATION

After collection, data were organized for analysis using the quantitative and qualitative methods. Data analysis refers to examining or scrutinizing the collected data or information in order to make inferences out of them. In

---

25. For an extensive description about the above methods, see Denscombe, *The Good Research Guide*, 133–227.

order to do that, the large mass of unorganized data (research information) were organized and broken into pieces for interpretation. In this study, both primary and secondary data were collected using tools elaborated above. The information was edited, summarized into respective objectives and the quantitative data were entered in a special program called Statistical Package for Social Sciences (SPSS) for analysis. The analyzed data were presented by the use of tables in order to make interpretations easy. For data which were collected through open-ended questionnaires, we grouped them, drew themes from them and discussed the themes in comparison with researches of other scholars.

Similarly, data from interviews were analyzed through recording the recurring themes and discussing in comparison with researches of other scholars. This means that in all aspects, our sole concern in the interpretation and discussion stages was to see how the obtained data proved or disproved the hypothesis formulated; and how the emerging themes related to the major issue of our study: the use of English language as a language of teaching and learning in Tanzania and how it affected student's academic performance in community secondary schools at the study area.

CONCLUSION

This chapter has discussed the procedure or the way in which the study was conducted from start to end. We have described the hypothesis to be confirmed or not confirmed by data from the field in regard to the proposition that the lack of adequate English language proficiency contributed to poor performance in community secondary schools in Tanzania. Moreover, the chapter has clarified the area of study and sources of data which are categorized as primary and secondary sources of data. The chapter has described the populations which were included in this study alongside their samples. Furthermore, the chapter has also explained the sampling design and methods employed during data collection, and how the collected data were analyzed and presented. Eventually, it has described how the implications and feedbacks were provided to the sampled informants.

When ending this chapter, we should say that there is, of course, no method without weaknesses however eminent it may be, and so is ours. Some of the weaknesses of our methodological perspective, as described in this chapter, are obvious: first, it does not clearly define the validity and reliability of both the instruments used for data collection and the collected data. Second, it does not clearly lay out the ethical issues which were involved in the study and how they were overcome; third, it does not clearly outline the limitations that hindered the proper execution of the study and how they were overcome so as to obtain the required data; and fourth, it does not discuss the theoretical perspective on which the whole study is based.[26] Despite the mentioned weaknesses, we are confident that the methodological perspective outlined in this chapter still provides an adequate direction to ascertain what was done in the research process leading to the production of this book.

---

26. Strictly speaking, the whole of this study is based on Paulo Freire's perspectives of Banking and Problem-Posing education. Freire, the Brazilian educator, distinguishes between "banking education" where learners have no contribution to what they receive from their teachers, and "problem-posing education" whereby students have room to articulate and reflect on what they receive. On the one hand, in baking education, learners are passive recipients of materials from their teachers (Freire, *Pedagogy of the Oppressed*, 52). Freire outlines ten characteristics of banking education: "a) the teacher teaches and the students are taught; b)the teacher knows everything and the students know nothing; c) the teacher thinks and the students are thought about; d) the teacher talks and the students listen–meekly; e) the teacher disciplines and the students are disciplined; f) the teacher chooses and enforces his choice, and the students comply; g) the teacher acts and the students have the illusion of acting through the action of the teacher; h) the teacher chooses the program content, and the students (who were not consulted) adopt to it; i) the teacher confuses the authority of knowledge with his or her professional authority, which she or he sets in opposition to the freedom of the students; j) the teacher is the Subject of the learning process, while the pupils are mere objects." (Freire, *Pedagogy of the Oppressed*, 54) Therefore, baking education kills the critical consciousness and creativity of students turning them into mere recipients and memorizers (instead of understanding) of what they receive.

On the other hand, "In problem-posing education, people develop their power to perceive critically *the way they exist* in the world *with which* and *in which* they find themselves; they come to see the world not as a static reality, but as a reality in process, in transformation." (Freire, *Pedagogy of the Oppressed*, 64; italics is in original). In this type of education, both teacher and learner are in the process of learning in the course of teaching. The teacher presents some materials to students to think critically on them and provide their own articulation, which leads the teacher towards re-thinking critically on the students' articulations (Freire, *Pedagogy of the Oppressed*, 62). Basing on Freire's theoretical perspective, though not fully outlined, we argue in our study that using English, a foreign language, as a medium of instruction encourages more banking education among Tanzanian students in all levels than problem-posing education.

Chapter 4

Hearing from Educational Stakeholders
Data Presentation and Discussion

> "... one of the major components of academic (scientific) method involves your ability to make a point through reasoning and evidence ... to convince readers that your point of view is correct and worth taking into account."
> —Mligo, Introduction to Research Methods, 117.

INTRODUCTION

Research is not complete by just reviewing the literatures, laying out the procedures of execution and collection of research data. Rather, it becomes complete, and makes its point, when research report is produced. It is through the report that the intended audience will be convinced and persuaded to believe in the argument, or reject it depending on the persuasive power it has and the way it makes sense of the informants' perspectives. The report can be either written or verbal report. However, the report cannot be produced, and the perspectives of informants be heard, if the collected data will be left in the form which they were collected from sources. Therefore, for our research to make its point, as Mligo states above, this chapter makes its point by presenting and discussing the perspectives of research informants (stakeholders) on the issue of English as a language of instruction in the Tanzanian context and the way it relates to students' academic performance in community secondary schools. What did they say about the use of English language as a language of instruction in community secondary schools basing on their experiences; and what does it mean to the current Tanzanian educational system? This is the basic question for this chapter.

However, as we move towards making sense of the informants' perspectives and their relevance to the Tanzanian educational system, it is important to understand what it means by the concept of *perspective* itself. The term *perspective* mentioned in the previous paragraph captures the whole idea of what we have done in this chapter in presenting the reality of the use of English language in Tanzanian secondary schools in relation to the question of academic performance. Why should one have a perspective in presenting the reality of a particular place? It is simply because reality is vast and difficult to grasp in its whole and can only be seen or understood through a particular perspective. Therefore, a perspective is an angle of vision to view a particular reality.[1] "In using the term *perspective* we simply mean a point of view, a way of looking at things ... a particular set of assumptions, beliefs and values on the part of the person holding the perspective which in turn will be influenced by the culture in which he [she] lives ... "[2] To present the perspectives from research informants, this chapter deals with three major aspects: it presents the obtained data, analyzes them, and discusses the findings in relation to the findings of similar researches from other researchers in regard to English as a language of instruction.

The chapter is divided into the following parts: the description of the research area, the provision of educational information, the presentation of teachers' and students' information and the presentation of form four students' performance in four sampled secondary schools. Moreover, the chapter provides responses from close-ended questionnaires in regard to knowledge of English among teachers and students, and students' academic performance. It also discusses the reasons for students' inability in English skills (writing, reading, speaking, and understanding) which makes them perform poorly at Form Four examinations. Eventually, the chapter provides some recommendations on what should be done to improve performance if English language will continue to be used as the LoI for secondary schools in Tanzania.

Basing on the obtained data and evidence from other researches, this chapter argues that students' failures in examinations in community secondary schools in Tanzania is mainly caused by the inability of both

1. Mligo, *Symbolic Interactionism*, 1–6.
2. Cohen & Manion, *Perspectives on Classrooms*, 1.

students and teachers to use English language as a language of teaching and learning as they move from Kiswahili, the commonly spoken language, to English, the language mostly used in classes. To use the words of Esch, the chapter demonstrates that "evidence of differences in English proficiency levels between students coming out of private schools and the public school sector . . . seems to be associated with teachers' levels of proficiency and training. It is also related to the availability and quality of materials used in schools. . . ."[3] Hence, after going through this chapter, our readers should be aware of the findings and determine themselves whether English language is still an appropriate LoI in the current Tanzanian context.

MBEYA DISTRICT COUNCIL AS AN AREA OF RESEARCH

Before presenting and discussing the findings of this study, we first describe the area where data were collected. In the previous chapter we just stated that Mbeya District Council was selected for research and promised to provide a detailed description of it in this findings chapter.[4] We also stated the reasons for selecting it to represent the various other parts of Tanzania which have community secondary schools. In this section we describe this area of research in a more detail to enable the readers better understand the collected data. According to data obtained in the District Office during fieldwork,[5] Mbeya District Council lies between 2300–2800m altitudes from above sea levels. The average temperature in this area ranges from 12° to 30° centigrade annually. The mean annual rainfall ranges between 1500mm and 2700mm. This range means that the area has adequate rainfall to enable inhabitants continue with agricultural activities well.

Topographically, the District is characterized by highlands, mountainous peaks, and lowlands of Songwe valley. The most predominant natural vegetation of this area includes Tropical, Savannah and wooded grasslands. Administratively, this district is divided into 3 divisions namely Tembela, Usongwe and Isangati. Moreover, it has 28 Wards and 143 villages with 1100 hamlets. The administrative division of this district is clearly shown in the table below.

3. Esch, "English and Empowerment," 8.

4. See the previous chapter of this book under the section of "Area of Study and Sources of Data."

5. The whole presentation of this section will depend mainly on the data obtained from this office.

Table 1: District Area, Number of Divisions, Wards, Villages and Hamlets

S/N	Division	Land Area Sq. Km	Number of wards	Number of villages	Number of hamlets
1	Tembela	1,216	10	55	361
2	Usongwe	391	10	40	335
3	Isangati	825	8	48	404
	Total	2,432	28	143	1,100

Source: *Field Work, September, 2016*

Administration and Land Area

The district lies between latitude 7° and 9° South of the Equator and between longitudes 33° and 35° East of the Greenwich. It borders Mbarali district to the East, Rungwe and Ileje districts to the South. The district is also bordered by Chunya district to the northwest. It also boarders Mbozi district to the west. Hence, Mbeya District Council exists in relation with other districts within and outside Mbeya Region.

The District has a total land area of 2,432 square kilometers, of which 189,818 acres is arable land ideal for agricultural production, while about 47,354 acres are covered by forests and 6,028 are water bodies as well as unusable land. It is, therefore, worthwhile to say that Mbeya District Council is full of resources which if properly used by people, they can help them to have development. The district has an ample fertile land and forests both natural and artificial, and is also supported by having enough water bodies.

Transport and Communication

One aspect which determines the development of people in a particular area is the presence or absence of infrastructures. Infrastructures include transport systems. Mbeya District Council has a moderately good road network services. It consists of gravel roads and earth roads, some of which are difficult to pass during rainy seasons. The road passable rate is 80 percent. The district is also privileged to have the Tanzania Zambia Railways Authority (TAZARA) rail passing from Kampirimposhi in Zambia to Dar es Salaam in Tanzania and is also served by two highways to Malawi and

Zambia. Mbeya District Council is also served by an international Airport of Songwe located at Songwe. Following this, we can confidently say that transportation is not a problem in Mbeya District Council because it has passable roads and TAZARA which are used by most people. However, the air transport is basically for the well to do people, both in Mbeya city and Mbeya District Council.

Apart from transport, communication systems are also encouraging within and outside the District Council. The District Council has a moderately good communication channel with other parts of the country predominantly through telephone services. Other communication services within the District Council are Televisions, Radios, Newspapers, Posts, Mobile phones, Faxes, and E-mails. Therefore, as seen above, Mbeya District Council is served by different communication channels making people's communication with other parts of the region and the country to be not a problem.

Water and Energy Supply

In the District 42 percent of the households are served by clean, but not safe water. However, it is expected that the services will be improved after the formation of the water Board at District level and committees at village levels under the District long-term plan. Therefore, the data above convinces us to conclude that water supply remains a problem in Mbeya District Council. As seen above only 42 percent of the people are served with clean and safe water. However, this problem is not only big in Mbeya District Council, but also in most other parts of the country.

Apart from water, energy supply is also inadequate in the District Council. About 4 percent of the households are served with thermo power while the rest use other sources of energy like firewood, charcoal, kerosene and wood. In this case, energy is one of the major problems of Mbeya District Council which requires immediate attention. Most of the people in the district use firewood and charcoal which has some detrimental impacts to the environment.

Socio-economic and Agricultural Information

The main tribes in Mbeya District are Safwa, Malila, Ndali, and Nyakyusa. Houses in Mbeya District are permanent, semi-permanent and temporary ones. Permanent houses are those constructed using blocks, burnt bricks and roofed with corrugated iron sheets whereas semi-permanent houses are those constructed using bricks which are not burnt and roofed with corrugated iron sheets. Temporary houses are those constructed using mud or woods and are roofed with grasses.

Unemployment rate among youth is high in the district. There is higher financial economic power among male adults although women are engaged in most of the farming activities and petty businesses. Gender inequality is still a problem, which results in heavy women workload. Consequently, Mbeya District Council is dwelt by many tribes; and the residents have different statuses contributing to different kinds of houses.

As stated before, the District Council has more than 2,164 squire kilometers which are arable land, used for cultivation of coffee, maize, beans, Irish potatoes, pyrethrum, wheat, vegetables, sunflowers, sweet potatoes, cotton, simsim, groundnuts, cassava and livestock keeping. It is hereby said that Mbeya District Council has vast arable land which is suitable for a variety of crops as indicated above. The climatic condition favors the growth of various crops.

Industries, Forests, and People's Population

Industries available in the District Council include, Mbeya Cement Company, Mbeya Textile industry, Inyala Quarry and other small-scale industries like grain milling and vegetable oil industries. Hence, the mentioned industries found in the district have helped to employ several people from Mbeya District Council, Mbeya region, and other parts of the country.

Natural and planted forests are available and harvested to produce timbers and logs being used as building materials and other uses. In almost all the three divisions, the areas are well planted with artificial forests consisting of trees such as eucalyptus and Cyprus. These trees have raised the income of the people of Mbeya District Council. People are advised to ensure that they use to the maximum the opportunity of having land which supports planting of such trees.

Based on the population census of 2012, Mbeya District Council had a population of 334,662 of which 174,584 were females and 160,078 males with annual birth rate of 2.7 percent and growth rate of 2.5 percent. The table below indicates the population distribution per division.

Table 2: Distribution of Population in Each Division

S/N	Division	Population
1	Tembela	83,666
2	Usongwe	133,865
3	Isangati	117,131
	Total	334,662

Source: *Field Notes, September, 2016*

Educational Information

Until the time when this research was done, Mbeya District Council had a total of 160 primary schools out of these 157 were owned by the government and three by the private sector. Moreover, the council had 45 secondary schools out of which a total of 28 were community secondary schools. These community secondary schools had a total number of 718 teachers and 10,548 students out of whom 4,652 were males and 5,896 were females. The standard ratio for teachers to students for secondary schools in Tanzania was 1:45. However, the data above show that Mbeya District Council had a ratio of 1:234.[6] This situation tells us about the possibility that there that poor academic performance is also contributed by this poor ratio of teachers to students. It is difficult for these few teachers to properly handle the large number of students in Mbeya District Council.

TEACHERS' AND STUDENTS' GENERAL RESPONSES

After discussing the situation of the District in various aspects as a research area, this section starts presenting and discussing the findings for the study. Below are students' and teachers' responses as obtained from four sampled secondary schools. The responses are in various areas which we inquired them. Some of these aspects include: name of school, age, Ward of residence, sex of the student, class, whether English is a contributing factor for their performance or not, and the ability to read, write, speak

---

6. Source: Fieldwork, September 2016 (DEO's Office).

and understand English language. The students' table below is followed by the teachers' table which consists of the following aspects: name of school, Ward, sex, subject which the teacher teaches, class, availability of books, whether teachers were enough or not, teachers experience, English language proficiency as a contributing factor to students' failure or not, and whether the teacher is fluent in English language or not. The following table indicates the overall responses obtained from students.[7]

---

7. The names of students who provided the response for each school, the names of schools, and their Wards are withheld. Only letters are used here to represent the names of schools.

Table 3: Overall Students' Responses Obtained from the Field

S/N	Secondary School	Age Years	Sex	Class	English	Read	Write	Speak	Understand
1	A	18–20	Female	Form Three	Yes	Poor	Poor	Poor	Poor
2	A	18–20	Female	Form Three	Yes	Poor	Poor	Poor	Poor
3	A	18–20	Male	Form Three	Yes	Good	Good	Good	Good
4	A	15–17	Male	Form Three	Yes	Poor	Poor	Poor	Poor
5	A	18–20	Male	Form Three	Yes	Poor	Poor	Poor	Poor
6	A	18–20	Male	Form Three	No	Good	Good	Good	Good
7	A	15–17	Female	Form Three	Yes	Poor	Good	Poor	Bad
8	A	15–17	Female	Form Three	Yes	Poor	Poor	Poor	Poor
9	A	18–20	Female	Form Three	Yes	Bad	Bad	Bad	Bad
10	A	15–17	Male	Form Three	Yes	Good	Good	Good	Good
11	A	12–14	Female	Form One	Yes	Bad	Bad	Bad	Bad
12	A	12–14	Male	Form One	Yes	Good	Good	Good	Good
13	A	12–14	Female	Form One	Yes	Poor	Poor	Poor	Poor
14	A	12–14	Male	Form One	Yes	Poor	Poor	Poor	Poor
15	A	15–17	Male	Form One	Yes	Poor	Poor	Poor	Poor
16	A	12–14	Female	Form One	Yes	Good	Good	Good	Good

S/N	Sec-ondary School	Age Years	Sex	Class	English	Read	Write	Speak	Understand
17	A	12–14	Female	Form One	Yes	Good	Good	Good	Good
18	A	15–17	Female	Form One	Yes	Poor	Poor	Poor	Poor
19	A	15–17	Male	Form One	Yes	Good	Good	Good	Good
20	A	15–17	Male	Form One	Yes	Poor	Poor	Poor	Poor
21	B	15–17	Female	Form Four	Yes	Good	Good	Good	Good
22	B	15–17	Female	Form Four	Yes	Poor	Poor	Poor	Poor
23	B	15–17	Female	Form Four	Yes	Poor	Poor	Poor	Poor
24	B	18–20	Female	Form Four	Yes	Good	Good	Good	Good
25	B	15–17	Female	Form Four	Yes	Good	Good	Good	Good
26	B	18–20	Female	Form Four	Yes	Bad	Bad	Bad	Bad
27	B	15–17	Male	Form Four	No	Good	Good	Good	Good
28	B	15–17	Male	Form Four	Yes	Poor	Poor	Poor	Poor
29	B	15–17	Female	Form Four	No	Good	Good	Good	Good
30	B	15–17	Female	Form Four	Yes	Good	Good	Good	Good
31	B	15 17	Male	Form Three	Yes	Poor	Poor	Poor	Poor
32	B	15–17	Male	Form Three	Yes	Good	Good	Good	Good
33	B	15–17	Male	Form Three	Yes	Poor	Poor	Poor	Poor

S/N	Secondary School	Age Years	Sex	Class	English	Read	Write	Speak	Understand
34	B	15–17	Female	Form Three	Yes	Good	Good	Good	Good
35	B	15–17	Male	Form Three	Good	Good	Good	Good
36	B	15–17	Male	Form Three	Yes	Good	Good	Good	Good
37	B	15–17	Female	Form Three	Yes	Poor	Poor	Poor	Poor
38	B	15–17	Female	Form Three	Yes	Poor	Poor	Poor	Poor
39	B	18–20	Male	Form Three	Yes	Good	Good	Good	Good
40	B	15–17	Male	Form Three	Yes	Poor	Poor	Poor	Poor
41	C	15–17	Male	Form Two	Yes	Poor	Poor	Poor	Poor
42	C	15–17	Male	Form Two	Yes	Good	Good	Good	Good
43	C	15–17	Female	Form Two	Yes	Bad	Bad	Bad	Bad
44	C	15–17	Female	Form Two	Yes	Good	Good	Good	Good
45	C	15–17	Female	Form Two	Yes	Poor	Poor	Poor	Poor
46	C	15–17	Female	Form Two	No	Good	Good	Good	Good
47	C	15–17	Female	Form Two	Yes	Poor	Poor	Poor	Poor
48	C	15–17	Female	Form Two	Yes	Good	Good	Good	Good
49	C	15–17	Male	Form Two	Yes	Poor	Poor	Poor	Poor
50	C	18–20	Male	Form Two	Yes	Good	Good	Good	Good

S/N	Secondary School	Age Years	Sex	Class	English	Read	Write	Speak	Understand
51	C	15–17	Male	Form Four	Yes	Good	Good	Good	Good
52	C	15–17	Female	Form Four	Yes	Good	Good	Good	Good
53	C	15–17	Female	Form Four	Yes	Good	Good	Good	Good
54	C	18–20	Male	Form Four	Yes	Poor	Poor	Poor	Poor
55	C	15–17	Female	Form Four	Yes	Poor	Poor	Poor	Poor
56	C	18–20	Male	Form Four	Yes	Poor	Poor	Poor	Poor
57	C	15–17	Female	Form Four	Yes	Good	Good	Good	Good
58	C	15–17	Female	Form Four	Yes	Poor	Poor	Poor	Poor
59	C	18–20	Male	Form Four	Yes	Poor	Poor	Poor	Poor
60	C	18–20	Male	Form Four	No	Good	Good	Good	Good
61	D	18–20	Female	Form Four	Yes	Poor	Poor	Poor	Poor
62	D	18–20	Female	Form Four	Yes	Bad	Bad	Bad	Bad
63	D	18–20	Female	Form Four	Yes	Poor	Poor	Poor	Poor
64	D	18–20	Female	Form Four	Yes	Good	Good	Good	Good
65	D	15–17	Female	Form Four	Yes	Good	Good	Good	Good
66	D	15–17	Female	Form Four	Yes	Very Good	Very Good	Very Good	Very Good
67	D	18–20	Male	Form Four	Yes	Poor	Poor	Poor	Poor

S/N	Secondary School	Age Years	Sex	Class	English	Read	Write	Speak	Understand
68	D	12–14	Male	Form Four	Yes	Very Good	Very Good	Very Good	Very Good
69	D	18–20	Male	Form Four	Yes	Poor	Poor	Poor	Poor
70	D	15–17	Female	Form Four	Yes	Good	Good	Good	Good
71	D	15–17	Female	Form Three	Yes	Poor	Poor	Poor	Poor
72	D	15–17	Male	Form Three	Yes	Good	Good	Good	Good
73	D	15–17	Male	Form Three	No	Poor	Poor	Poor	Poor
74	D	15–17	Male	Form Three	Yes	Good	Good	Good	Good
75	D	15–17	Male	Form Three	Yes	Poor	Poor	Poor	Poor
76	D	12–14	Female	Form One	Yes	Good	Good	Good	Good
77	D	12–14	Male	Form One	Yes	Poor	Poor	Poor	Poor
78	D	12–14	Female	Form One	Yes	Poor	Poor	Poor	Poor
79	D	12–14	Male	Form One	Yes	Poor	Poor	Poor	Poor
80	D	12–14	Female	Form One	No	Good	Good	Good	Good
	Total			80	80	80	80	80	80

Source: *Field Work, September,* **2016**

Table 3 above shows a list of respondents from four secondary schools which are in three Wards of Ijombe, Inyala, and Utengule Usongwe. The table has 10 columns which consist of serial numbers, letter representing the secondary school, age range of respondents, sex of respondent, class, and response as to whether English has impact on student's performance; the last four columns contain responses as to whether the student could read, write, listen and understanding English. Discussions of each item will be done later after this general presentation when the presentation of individual tables will be done.

The following table indicates the overall responses obtained from the field in regard to teachers' responses to questions asked during field work.[8]

---

8. The names of individual teachers, their respective schools, and Wards are withheld. Only letters are used to represent their schools.

Table 4: Overall Teachers' Responses Obtained from the Field

S/N	Name of Secondary School	Sex	Subject of the teacher	Class of Student	Book availability	Teachers enough	Teachers experience	English proficiency	English fluency
1	X	Male	History	Form Three	No	No	3–5 years	Yes	No
2	X	Female	Book-Keeping	Form Four	No	No	6–9 years	Yes	No
3	X	Female	Biology	Form Three	Yes	No	3–5 years	Yes	No
4	X	Male	History	Form One	No	No	Over 10	Yes	No
5	X	Female	Geography	Form Two	No	No	3–5 years	Yes	No
6	X	Male	History	Form One	Yes	No	3–5 years	Yes	Yes
7	Y	Female	English	Form Four	No	No	3–5 years	Yes	No
8	Y	Male	Civics	Form Three	No	No	6–9 years	Yes	No
9	Y	Male	English	Form Four	No	No	3–5 years	Yes	No
10	Y	Male	English	Form Four	No	No	3–5 years	Yes	No
11	Y	Male	Kiswahili	Form Three	No	No	1–2 years	Yes	No
12	Y	Male	French	Form Three	No	No	6–9 years	Yes	No

13	Z	Female	Geography	Form Two	No	No	3–5 years	Yes	No
14	Z	Male	Kiswahili	Form Two	No	No	1–2 years	Yes	No
15	Z	Female	English	Form Three	No	No	6–9 years	Yes	Yes
16	Z	Male	Civics	Form Two	No	No	3–5 years	Yes	Yes
17	Z	Male	Geography	Form One	No	No	3–5 years	Yes	Yes
18	Z	Male	Geography	Form Two	No	No	3–5 years	No	Yes
19	H	Female	English	Form Two	No	No	3–5 years	Yes	No
20	H	Male	Economics	Form Four	No	No	Over 10yrs	Yes	No
21	H	Female	Chemistry	Form One	No	No	1–2 years	Yes	Yes
22	H	Female	History	Form Two	No	No	6–9 years	Yes	No
23	H	Male	Biology	Form Two	No	No	3–5 years	Yes	No
24	H	Male	Kiswahili	Form Three	No	No	6–9 years	Yes	No
Total		24	24	24	24	24	24	24	24

Source: *Field Work, September,* **2016**

English as a Language of Teaching and Learning

Table 4 above shows the list of teachers who responded to questionnaires about the use of English as a teaching and learning medium in community secondary schools of Usongwi, Nsongwi Juu, Imezu and Iwalanje within Mbeya District Council. The table has ten columns, from left is a serial number, letter representing the school, sex, subject which the teacher teaches, class, books availability, teachers enough or not, teachers experience, a response as to whether English language impacts student's understanding; and lastly, it is a column showing whether the teacher can teach students in English fluently without code switching and code mixing.[9] However, the discussions of each item will be done later in the following subsections.

PERFORMANCE IN FORM FOUR SUMMATIVE EXAMINATIONS

After presenting the overall responses of teachers, the table below presents the overall performance history of Mbeya District Council for three consecutive years from 2013, 2014, and 2015 in the respective community secondary schools which we conducted this study. The trend really indicates the performance of Mbeya DC against the number of students within those years.

---

9. Cf. Probyn, "Teachers' Voices"; Kinyaduka & Kiwara, "Language of Instruction," 95; Modupeola, "Code-Switching as a Teaching Strategy," 92–93.

Table 5: Overall Performance of Students in the Sampled Secondary Schools

School	Division I			Division II			Division III			Division IV			Division 0		
	2013	2014	2015	2013	2014	2015	2013	2014	2015	2013	2014	2015	2013	2014	2015
Z Sec School	1	0	0	3	4	1	11	5	1	37	23	20	40	39	38
X Sec. School	-	-	0	-	-	0	-	-	3	-	-	15	-	-	11
Y Sec. School	1	2	0	4	3	5	15	18	19	65	38	73	48	25	58
H Sec. School	3	2	1	12	16	16	17	40	52	119	90	137	54	26	88
Total	4	4	1	19	23	22	43	62	75	221	151	245	142	90	195
Total for Div	9			64			180			514			427		
Percentage	1%			5%			15%			43%			36%		

Source: *Field Work, September, 2016*

Table 5 above shows students' performance at Form Four National Examinations from four sampled secondary schools for three consecutive years. The data presented above indicate that very few students (9 students) scored division One which is 1%, 64 students scored division Two which is 5%, 180 students scored division Three which is 15%. The majority of students (514 students which is 43%) scored division Four whereby there was another big number of students (427 students which is 36%) fall under division zero. Hence, from the data above, the majority of students in the sampled community secondary schools scored division four and zero. In fact, this is very unwelcoming for the betterment of their life and the welfare of Tanzania as a country.

It should be remembered that students who acquire division One, Two, and Three can join Advanced level secondary education and are also eligible for various courses in certificate studies. Students in division Four and zero cannot be admitted to valuable certificates particularly in public collages. These are considered to be failures. Surprisingly, as presented above, these are the majority in the sampled schools. The question is: What was the main cause of this massive failure of students in their form four examinations in the sampled community secondary schools? In chapter one, we hypothesized that the use of English language as a medium for teaching and learning is the main cause of poor performance. The following sections of this chapter examine the validity of this hypothesis by discussing the individual aspects of the general findings presented in the two tables above.

THE STUDY AND USE OF ENGLISH: RESPONSES FROM CLOSE-ENDED QUESTIONNAIRES

In the following parts, we present and discuss data from close-ended questionnaires. We also provide an analysis of the data and some views on the various situations of teachers and students in relation to the use of English language for teaching and learning. Consequently, under this subtopic, several tables produced by the Special Package for Social Sciences (SPSS) programme are presented and discussed on each of the areas of our interests.

English Language and Academic Performance

In table 6 below, we present data from the field in which we wanted to know whether the poor English knowledge was a contributing factor to poor performance at Form Four in community secondary schools. The responses for this aspect are recorded below.

Table 6: Poor Knowledge of English as a Contributing Factor to Poor Performance

Responses	English Knowledge vs Performance			
	Frequency	Percent	Percent	Cumulative Percent
Yes	73	91.3	91.3	91.3
No	7	8.8	8.8	100
Total	80	100	100	

Source: *Field Work, September,* **2016**

Table 6 above shows responses from students in the surveyed schools on the question asked to determine whether the poor knowledge of English had a positive or negative impact on students' performance at Form Four examinations. The result indicates that 73 (91.3%) out of 80 respondents accepted that English affected students' performance negatively. Similar responses were obtained in the research by Ndalichako and Komba in some community secondary schools in Tanzania.

In a focused group discussion in one Tanzanian school of their research, one student confessed: "I think the major factor which contributes to massive failure rate in this school is the use of English language. Many students in the school do not speak English when they find English in Examinations they fail to respond to questions and sometimes they don't even understand the demand of the question. So they end up answering different things from what they have actually been asked. . . . "[10] Ndalichako and Komba's findings indicate that poor knowledge of English is one of the main causes for student's inability to respond to examination questions rightly, hence their failure.

At this point, we agree with Pitman, Majhanovich, and Brock-Utne that "Children should not be forced to learn in a language that they do not understand well."[11] Their statement comes from an extensive research in Tanzania and South Africa which discovered that most students in the two countries had better performance as they used their mother tongues in

---

10. Ndalichako and Komba, "Students' Subject Choice," 54.
11. Pitman, Majhanovich, and Brock-Utne, "English as a Language of Instruction," 3.

studying the subject contents. Instead, using a foreign language forced them to memorize the notes provided by their teachers, which thereafter were reproduced in the examinations without understanding what they meant. In fact this memorization of the taught content only for regurgitation in examinations hardly enables students to use the memorized knowledge in their life after they complete studies because it has not been internalized.[12]

Mwipopo's research confirms the above statement through his qualitative research among students in secondary schools. He quotes one student recalling thus in regard to what teachers do: "What are the teachers doing? So, a chemistry teacher—teaching in Kiswahili, giving the students notes that they write for students to copy, which are in English! And then they will have to answer the exams in English. The notes that they copy are for memorizing, they [students] don't know anything! So remember they cannot pick a book and read for themselves and find out some knowledge."[13] The student's statement indicates the way the current educational skills and Tanzanians' ability to think and articulate issues is jeopardized by the incompetent teachers. Students are there to memorize materials, regurgitate on papers during examinations and acquire marks, which eventually provide them descent certificates; in that case, students are mostly prepared to have descent certificates, not descent servants of the Tanzanian society.

English Language and Ages of Respondents

The poor knowledge of English discussed above is mainly contributed by the age which students are fully exposed to the language. The age of our respondents was divided into four major groups, from 12 to 14 years, from 15 to 17 years and from 18 to 20 years and lastly students above 20 years. The table below indicates clearly this age division.

Table 7: Ages of Respondents

Age of Respondent				
Years	Frequency	Percent	Percent	Cumulative Percent
From 12–14	12	15	15	15

12. Babaci-Wilhite & Geo-Jaja, "Localization of Instruction," 8.
13. Mwipopo, "Secondary School Graduates' Personal Experiences," 146.

From 15-17	48	60	60	75
From 18-20	20	25	25	100
Total	80	100	100	

Source: *Field Work, September, 2016*

In table 7 above, the data are concerned about ages of respondents. The question here was this: is the age of respondents a factor for students' low ability to grasp English as a language of teaching and learning? The above table shows that most of our respondents were between 15 to 17 years (60%). This is the most active age in the life of humanity. There were no students above 20 years, and hence people with age above 20 do not appear in the table above. This told us that though the researched group was in an active age in terms of life in general, this age was a determining factor for their failure to use English language.

Research results by Gawi in Saudi Arabia indicate that the appropriate age for children to study a foreign language is between 5 and 6 years. Studying the language at an advanced age becomes difficult and hard to grasp.[14] Following Gawi's findings, we can say that the age of community secondary school students studied above is inappropriate as a suitable age for active learning of the language. Makgato states that "A popular belief is that the sooner the child is exposed to English in the classroom, the better he/she will learn the language."[15] In the statement of the problem in chapter one of this book, we stated that the movement from the more internalized Kiswahili language in the early childhood to a foreign English language is not only an abrupt shift, but also a bottleneck to the understanding of both the foreign English language and the taught content of the various subject.

English Language and Availability of Books

Availability of teaching and learning materials is one of the most important aspects for successful instruction. Availability of books is a single most important thing that cannot be avoided if we want to improve the status of education in community secondary schools. Table 8 below indicates responses from the schools visited on whether books were available or not.

---

14. Gawi, "The effects of Age Factor," 129–130.
15. Cf. Makgato, "The Use of English," 234.

Table 9: Availability of Books

	Availability of Books			
	Frequency	Percent	Percent	Cumulative Percent
Yes	2	8.3	8.3	8.3
No	22	91.7	91.7	100
Total	24	100	100	

Source: *Field Work, September,* 2016

Table 8 above shows responses from teachers in regard to the availability of books and other learning and teaching materials. Out of 24 teachers who responded to our questionnaires, 22 (91.7%) said books were not enough in their schools, while only 2 (8.3%) said the books were enough. Consequently, the unavailability of books contributed to their inability to use English as they lacked reading materials. Similar results were obtained in a qualitative research conducted by Makunja in some community secondary schools in Morogoro Tanzania. In her interview with one of the academic masters of the surveyed schools on the factors hindering the implementation of Competent-Based Curriculum, the academic master had the following to share: "The textbooks are not enough to satisfy the increased number of students. In our school, book-student ratio ranges from 1:7 to 1:10. But in other schools the situation is even worse so you can imagine how challenging the situation can be...."[16]

Furthermore, one of the heads of researched community secondary schools commented that even the available books, especially those written by private authors, encouraged more memorization and creaming than creative thinking and argumentation: "Most of the books produced by private writers are of low quality and some of them are in forms of question and answers. Unfortunately, students prefer reading books with questions and answers which make them learn by memorizing and cramming. This limits their ability to learn through discovery and problem-solving."[17] This statement from the head of school suggest for the banking education being

---

16. Makunja, "Challenges facing Teachers," 32; cf. John, "What is the Difference?" 59–60.

17. Ibid., cf. Wilson & Komba, "The Link between English Language," 3–4; Mwipopo, "Secondary School Graduates' Personal Experiences," 160–161.

encouraged to students in most secondary schools in Tanzania through the types of available books they use.

Following the above results, Pitman, Majhanovich and Brock-Utne are probably right when they write: "The lack of resources in the various mother tongues has also been cited as an excuse not to use the mother tongue as the medium of instruction."[18] The data presented above suggest that for smooth learning, the availability of both teaching and learning materials is extremely important. Moreover, Rugemalira also reports that lack of English books for English medium schools, and the resurgence of Kiswahili books instead, is one of the hindrances towards students' understanding of what they learn in these schools using English.[19] In this case, where students have confessed to be running in shortage of books, it is difficult to expect effective learning and teaching. The question here is whether Tanzania should continue using the language whose teaching materials are scarce, and those available encourage banking education instead of problem posing one.

We support the idea by Rugemalira on the importance of materials and supplies for improving the teaching and learning activity, if English continues to be the LoI for secondary schools in Tanzania, because in those materials, especially books, is where the knowledge of the subject matter emerges. Hence, it is confidently said that, there is no way students can perform better at any school if there are no text and reference books for them to review. Teachings from teachers alone can hardly be sufficient to help students pass their examinations. It is indicated by this research that unavailability of appropriate books in community secondary schools is another great contributing factor to students' failure at Form Four level examinations.

English Language and Teachers' Availability

Teachers are the pillars in the teaching and learning process. Students can have everything at their disposal, but if there are no teachers to lead the learning way, it will be difficult for them to have effective learning process. The table below indicates teachers' availability in community secondary schools visited for study.

---

18. Pitman, Majhanovich and Brock-Utne, "English as a Language of Instruction," 3.
19. Rugemalira, "Theoretical and Practical Challenges," 75–76.

Table 9: Teachers Availability

	Teachers Enough			
	Frequency	Percent	Percent	Cumulative Percent
No.	24	100	100	100

Source: *Field Work, September, 2016*

Table 9 above indicates responses from teachers of the visited secondary schools on the question as to whether teachers were enough in their respective schools or not. In their views, all the 24 teachers (100%) had opinions that teachers were not enough in their schools. This situation was obviously based on the well-known ratio of one teacher to forty five students (1:45). Therefore, since all the respondents disclosed that teachers were not enough in their schools, it follows, therefore, that it was difficult for effective instruction to happen in these schools.

Similar results were obtained by Mlay. In her research in two community secondary schools in Arusha Tanzania (one urban and other rural), it was found that the schools had no enough teachers in regard to the number of students enrolled in those schools. The number of students in an urban secondary school was 183 while in the rural one was 225. In her interview with the rural secondary school teachers, it was related to her that the teacher-student ratio in that rural school was 1:70–75. This ratio indicates that the number of teachers in the surveyed school was not proportional to the number of students being enrolled.[20]

However, teachers' availability must go hand in hand with their commitment to teach as Evans and Brueckner reveal: "to be successful in any profession, it is necessary to acquire and maintain a deep commitment to that profession. A strong commitment is especially critical for teachers because what they do on the job, or fail to do, directly affect the lives of students".[21] Evans and Brueckner's idea is valid and convincing; it is convincing because falling short of teachers' commitment to the profession makes it difficult for them to teach properly. If teachers are not teaching well, because of lack of commitment, students are expected to fail in their studies.

---

20. Mlay, "The Influence of the Language of Instruction," 53–54.
21. Evans and Brueckner, *Teaching and You*, 120.

Emphasizing on this idea of commitment, Myra and Sandker say that historically, the demand for new teachers has resembled a roller coaster ride. Myra and Sandker write: "The teaching shortage meant virtually anyone would be hired as a teacher, with or without the proper credentials."[22] We agree with this statement since most of our schools, particularly community secondary schools in the research area, and in Tanzania as a whole, run in short of teachers. It is no wonder to find a school in rural areas with three or four teachers while students are many making the ratio of teacher to students very un-proportional. This being the case, it is certain that the availability of teachers is one of the most important aspects in the learning process. Teachers are students' leaders; in fact, they are more than leaders. There cannot be learning where there are no teachers even if everything is available. Hence, the government has the responsibility to ensure that Tanzanian schools, community, private, and public, are not short of teachers.

English Language and Teachers' Teaching Experiences

Working experience is another most important factor for effective teaching. Job advertisements often have an element requiring applicants with long working experiences who can perform their duties thoroughly and efficiently. It is true that a person with a long working experience can be better than a person who is new to the job or position. The table below documents the experiences of teachers at our research area.

Table 10: Teachers' Experience

	Teachers Experience			
Years	Frequency	Percent	Percent	Cumulative Percent
1–2 years	3	12.5	12.5	12.5
3–5 years	13	54.2	54.2	66.7
6–9 years	6	25	25	91.7
Over 10 years	2	8.3	8.3	100
Total	24	100	100	

Source: *Field Work, September,* 2016

22. Myra & Sadker, *Teachers, Schools and Society*, 542.

Table 10 above shows teachers working experiences in terms of years. As you can see from the table, a large number of teachers are those with an experience of between 3–5 years (54.2%). Together with other factors, effective teaching and learning depends on teachers' experience. It is expected that teachers who are more experienced can properly help students to better perform at different levels of their study. It is unfortunate that the sampled community secondary schools had very few long experienced teachers. Teachers who have worked for over 10 years accounted for only 8.3%. It goes beyond doubt that long experience contributes to efficiency if everything is constant. In addition, there were few teachers who worked from 1–2 years.

It is believed that this may have been caused by the fact that teachers are government employees and the government has one employment season for teachers which was effected over one year ago. Evans and Brueckner cement on what we have discussed above when they assert that one of the very important qualities of a good teacher is experience. Experience plays as grounding for the accumulated exposure to the problems of teaching and how to solve them through the use of various methods. Teachers with a long experience will try an activity using a certain method and when they fail, they can always try another one.[23] It is for this reason that we argued that since most teachers in the sampled area fell between 3–5 years of teaching, it is assumed that this is a contributing factor to students' failures since the schools do not have long experienced teachers.

English Language Proficiency and Students' Failure in Examinations

Both students and teachers were asked about English proficiency vis-à-vis students' failure at Form Four examinations. The intention was to determine whether the knowledge of English language (writing, reading, speaking and understanding) contributed to poor or better performance at Form Four examinations in the respective community secondary schools.

---

23. Evans and Brueckner, *Teaching and You.*

Table 11: English Proficiency and Students' Failure

English Proficiency as a Cause of Students Failure			
Response	Frequency	Percent	Percent	Cumulative Percent
Yes	23	95.8	95.8	95.8
No	1	4.2	4.2	100
Total	24	100	100	

Source: *Field Work, September, 2016*

The table 11 above shows the responses to the question as to whether English proficiency had an impact on students' performance. A total of 23 teachers (95.8%) out of 24 teachers agreed that English proficiency was a cause of students' failure in community secondary schools. Only 1 teacher (4.2%) said English proficiency had no contribution on students' performance. According to our experiences as researchers, English has great negative impacts to students' learning and understanding of what they learn.

Similar results with the above were obtained by Mwipopo's research. In his qualitative research in one of the Tanzanian schools quoted one student who said: "I think the disadvantage is that it [English] causes some students to drop out of school. I know some of my friends who failed the form two national exam and they never came back. I think it is because of the English language. There's no point of going back to school when they cannot communicate with teachers and friends. Many people don't need English in Tanzania. Me, I think for most Tanzanians, English is a waste of time. Many Tanzanians don't need English...."[24]

In fact, it costs most teachers to code-switch when they teach in order to enable students understand. One teacher in Tanzania was quoted by Mwajuma Siama Vuzo saying that teachers face difficulties to make students understand what they teach when using English as a language of instruction. The teacher said: "Most of the students do not understand.... we have to develop classroom management strategies like code-switching and translation.... students fail, not because they are dull but because they have a barrier in their use and understanding of the English language..."[25]

---

24. Mwipopo, "Secondary School Graduates' Personal Experiences," 141.

25. Vuzo in Brock-Utne & Desai, "Expressing Oneself," 12; cf. Modupeola, "Code-Switching as a Teaching Strategy," 92–93.

Code switching of language among students and teachers in academic interactions is a serious issue in Tanzanian secondary schools, whether government, private or community secondary schools. Mwajuma Vuzo conducted a mainly qualitative research cf to determine the extent of code switching and/or code mixing in two Tanzanian government secondary schools. Target students were the form one, a group of students that had just joined secondary level education from both English and Kiswahili medium primary schools. According to Vuzo, the following were the reasons provided by students when they code-switched from English to Kiswahilli:

- "*Tunatumia mchanganyiko . . . tunaogopa kuchekwa tukikosea English* . . . We use both English and Kiswahili because we are scared of being laughed at when we make mistakes in English.
- *Tunatumia Kiswahili darasani kuuliza maswali ili kupata maana na kuelewa zaidi . . .* We use Kiswahili in class to ask questions so as to get meaning and to understand more.
- *Tunatumia Kiswahili darasani ili kuelekezana maneno magumu. . . .* We use Kiswahili in class so as to explain to each other the difficult words.
- *Natumia Kiswahili ninaposhindwa kutunga sentensi kwa Kiingereza* . . . I use Kiswahili especially when I cannot construct a sentence in English."[26]

According to the students' above responses, students code-switch from English to Kiswahili most likely because they see "Kiswahili [to be] the matrix language and English is the embedded language."[27] This means that Kiswahili is viewed to be the main language that plays a significant role towards their understanding of the taught content; and English plays a minor role.

Mwipopo obtained similar results to those of Vuzo. In his qualitative research, Mwipopo quotes a student confessing to have a difficulty to learn English language because of fear of being laughed. The student says: "The difficult part for me was trying to learn English in front of other students, and people laugh at you, if you said the words not in the right way. That was a daunting part for me."[28]

---

26. Vuzo, "Stakeholders' Opinions," 135; cf. Brock-Utne, "English as the Language of Instruction," 3–11 (Italics is in the original).

27. Ibid.

28. Mwipopo. "Secondary School Graduates Personal Experiences," 140; cf. Mlay, "The Influence of the Language of Instruction," 13.

Furthermore, in the research by Brock-Utne and Desai using cartoons, whereby students in some Tanzanian schools were asked to write a story about them, they showed a generally low proficiency in expressing themselves in English.[29] Though, in their research, there was a discrepancy in English proficiency depending on the level of study, with form one level having the lowest and form six having the highest, their research generally indicates that English is still a problem to Tanzanian students in various levels of study. The problem arises due to small vocabulary as most students move from their native language in primary schools to a foreign language. Hence, Mulokozi further emphasizes that "Teaching these levels [secondary and even higher education levels] is still . . . conducted in broken English, though in practice most teachers in secondary schools resort to Kiswahili to make themselves understandable."[30]

Furthermore, a research by Ndalichako and Komba presents the responses from students themselves as primary interlocutors of learning. In their research, a student confessed to understand better when Kiswahili was used than when English was used: "I like Kiswahili because it is our national language and I understand the teacher better than I do in subjects taught in English. . . . "[31] Therefore, in line with the arguments above, all education stakeholders including teachers, parents and students themselves have to ensure that deliberate efforts are made to improve the English proficiency as a foreign language of instruction to students in community secondary schools; if it continues to be the LoI at all. Otherwise, using a language which students show a good command of it, such as Kiswahili as the student confessed above, would be more appropriate if the Tanzanian government is serious towards making a stride in students' mastery of what they learn and enhancing a critical mind to students.[32]

29. Brock-Utne and Desai, "Experiencing Oneself," 19.
30. Mulokozi, "Kiswahili as a National and International Language," 72.
31. Ndalichako and Komba, "Students' Subjects Choice," 54.
32. Arvi Hurskainen is caught with a wonder as to why Tanzanian people, especially Government leaders concerned with education have been struggling to resort to English, a foreign language which students hardly grasp fully what they learn. In his words, Hurskainen writes in Kiswahili: *"Nasema tu kwa kifupi na wazi kwamba kwangu binafsi ni vigumu kuelewa kwa nini Mtanzania yeyote, sembuse viongozi wa elimu, wangependa kurudisha nyuma maendeleo ya elimu kwa kujaribu kuingiza Kiingereza badala ya Kiswahili kama lugha ya kufundishia."* [Literal translation: I just say in short and openly that to me personally it is difficult to understand as to why any Tanzanian, and especially leaders of education, would like to push back the development of education by trying to impose English as a language of instruction instead of Kiswahili] (Hurskainen, "Kiswahili na

English as a Language of Teaching and Learning

Teachers' Fluency in English Language

In speaking about the English language fluency of teachers as educators, as far as the findings of this research are concerned, we have to first consider the words of Sharma who writes: "To educate the educator—that is, to have him [her] understand himself [herself]—is one of the most difficult undertaking, because most of us are already cristalized within a system of thought or pattern of action; we have given ourselves over to some ideology, to a religion, or to a particular standard of conduct. That is why we teach the child *what* to think and not how to think."[33] Students learn many things from teachers (educators). Among other things, they learn about word formation, pronunciations, vocabularies, reading, writing and speaking from their teachers. It is with this understanding that all teachers are supposed to be fluent in English regardless of what subject they teach. This is basically because currently the medium of instruction in secondary schools is English language.

What is the situation to the community secondary schools in the surveyed area during this study? The table below provides responses in regard to teachers' fluency in English language in the schools visited for study.

Table 12: Teachers Fluency in English

	Teachers Fluency in English			
	Frequency	Percent	Percent	Cumulative Percent
Yes	6	25.0	25.0	25.0
No	18	75.0	75.0	100.0
Total	24	100.0	100.0	

Source: *Field Work, September,* **2016**

Hali Halisi," 115).

Hurskainen's wonder above suggests that the educational leadership in Tanzania has possibly not been serious enough with what it says and what it implements in terms of language of instruction. Politically, it speaks of Kiswahili as the sole cultural language to be used in all spheres of Tanzanians, including the secondary and higher education sector, while practically emphasizes the use of English in all important sectors such as higher education, high court activities, diplomacy, science and technology, and international trade (cf. Msanjila, "Hali ya Kiswahili katika Shule za Sekondari," 207; Yoradi, "Lugha ya Kiswahili katika Kufundishia," 21–23).

33. Sharma, *Problems of Education,* 149–150.

Hearing from Educational Stakeholders

The question intended to know how fluent in English language teachers were when in the classroom. We wanted to assess whether teachers fluently used English language while teaching. Table 12 above shows that 18 teachers (75%) used Kiswahili language in teaching various subjects because they were not fluent in English themselves. It is only 6 respondents (25%) who said that they could use English in teaching students without any problem. Similar results were obtained from Mwajuma Vuzo's research in the two government schools. In her research Vuzo found that most teachers code-switched the language of instruction from English to Kiswahili either making it as a coping strategy to enable students understand the taught content or as a result of lack of adequate fluency.

When asked whether they code-switched when teaching, two of the teachers had the following responses: The first said:

> *Ndio, mimi nachanganya lugha, mfano wanafunzi wanakutazama tu, hawaitiki, au wanaitika kwa wasiwasi . . . saa nyingine umefundisha kitu unapouliza swali hawajibu. Hivyo inabidi niwasaidie wanafunzi kwa kutoa mifano, kuchora na vilevile kusisitiza.* Yes, I do CS [Code–Switch], for instance, when students stare at you and do not respond to questions and if they do, they do so with great uncertainty which you can tell from the tone of their voices . . . sometimes you have taught something after which you ask a question and no one responds. In this case, I am forced to code switch to Kiswahili to help them understand by giving them realistic examples, drawings and stressing points."[34]

The second teacher had these words:

> *Naona umuhimu wa kuchanganya lugha katika vipindi kwa sababu . . . wanafunzi wanaonekana kutokuelewa somo na kutokushiriki darasani . . . saa nyingine pia na mimi mwenyewe napungukiwa na maneno ya kujieleza vizuri.* I find it important to use code switching in class because students seem not to have understood the lesson and they are not active and at times I experience being short of words to express myself well in English."[35]

---

34. Vuzo, "Stakeholders' Opinions," 135.

35. Ibid., 139. For examples on how teachers code switch and code mix in classrooms, please see Kadeghe, "Code-Switching in Tanzanian Classrooms," 118-122. For similar results in South African schools on the issue of code switching of teachers when in classrooms because of failure of students to understand what they teach, please see Makgato, "The Use of English," 937.

English as a Language of Teaching and Learning

The above research results and quotations from Vuzo show how much students in most Tanzanian secondary schools are deprived of the right to learn from their teachers because they themselves, due to inability to use English, use Kiswahili most of their time when in classes. Students have very little or no opportunity to learn from their teachers who code-switch to Kiswahili to hide their lack of adequate fluency in English language while using students as scapegoats for the blame. Snow emphasizes that English teachers must be fluent in the Language and experienced in teaching it if they are to help their students at all.[36]

Moreover, another research by Mwipopo testifies the wider extent of the problem of English, not only to teachers at secondary schools, but also to colleges and universities. One student was quoted in his research saying: "Today, as you know even in colleges in Tanzania, at the university, students have a hard time using English. Even teaching English at the university is problematical. You know, the teachers have to mix in Swahili and English. A lot of teachers are not even competent to teach in English themselves, you know. Things have drastically declined. Nobody who is honest can dispute it. . . . "[37]

On top of that, one university lecturer in the resent research by Lupogo stated that the background of English from primary school was the cause of the poor English to most university lecturers as they moved to secondary and then Universities. In the own words, the lecturer was quoted saying: "we do not have a strong English background, as you can reflect back to primary education which uses Kiswahili as Language of instruction. At that early age is when a pupil can acquire or learn a language effortlessly and easily. Although English is taught as the subject, sometimes you can find even the English teacher is not competent. Then, what do you expect?"[38] What do the student and lecturer say in the above statements? Possibly, the student and the lecturer say that English language is problematic to the whole system of education in Tanzania from the kindergarten to university level.

Here we find Sharma's questions important. Sharma says: "The first thing the teacher must ask himself [herself], when he [she] decides that he [she] wants to teach, is what exactly he [she] means by teaching. . . . Does he [she] wants [sic!] to condition the child to become a cog in the social machine, or help him [her] to be an integrated, creative human being, a

36. Snow, *From Language Learner to Language Teacher*.
37. Mwipopo, "Secondary School Graduates Personal Experiences," 148–149.
38. Lupogo, "The Intensity of Language of Instruction," 50.

threat to false values? . . . If one [the teacher] is blind, can one help others to cross to the other shore?"[39]

It is our opinion that, since the government still holds on English as LoI, teachers in all levels of education should have a good mastery of English language to help their students understand the content they teach them. There is also a necessity of having experienced teachers as Snow has just proposed. Here, competent teachers are required, those who have spent a considerable time studying and learning foreign languages, and who are knowledgeable about both the language and the subject being taught. However, the question still remains: How can the country have English language competent teachers while most of the ones we currently have also passed through a similar situation as that which their students are currently passing? They themselves did not understand from their teachers, who also did not understand from their teachers. This means that the whole system of education should be revisited!

KNOWLEDGE OF ENGLISH LANGUAGE AND STUDENTS' ACADEMIC PERFORMANCE

Having discussed about students' and teachers' general proficiency in English as a language of teaching and learning, this sub-section deals with the knowledge of English in the four major skills: understanding, speaking, reading, and writing as reported in the research data and in comparison with other similar researches.

Students' Ability to Read English Language

The first aspect is the students' ability to read English. The table below shows the students' ability to read English:

---

39. Sharma, *Problems of Education*, 152.

Table 13: Ability to Read English

	Reading English			
Responses	Frequency	Percent	Percent	Cumulative Percent
Very Good	2	2.5	2.5	2.5
Good	35	43.8	43.8	46.3
Poor	38	47.5	47.5	93.8
Bad	5	6.3	6.3	100
Total	80	100	100	

Source: *Field Work, September, 2016*

In table 13 above, we wanted to know the ability of students to read English. The results were that 38 respondents (47%) said they were poor in reading English whereas 2 (2.5%) of our respondents said they could read English very well, and 35 (43.8%) respondents said that they were good at reading English, and 5 (6.3%) of our respondents said that they are bad in reading English. As the data indicate above, most of the students could not read English properly; and if they could not read, that means they were unquestionably unable to understand the written content of what is taught to them; and hence, they were eligible to failing in their Form Four final examinations.

The data above clearly show that most students in the sampled schools and classes had problems in reading English, see the 47% of students who said they were poor in reading English. Knowledge in reading English has a close connection to students academic performance at any level, be it Form Four, Form six or Form Two. A similar result was obtained from the qualitative research conducted by Makunja to some community secondary schools at Morogoro Tanzania about the challenges in implementing Competent–Based Curriculum in those schools. In an interview with one of the Academic Mistresses of Schools, the Mistress said: "Low quality of students is a big challenge to us. The majority of the students who are selected to join secondary schools, especially community-based secondary schools like ours do not qualify . . . they have low academic ability so it becomes difficult to assist them especially, when you rely on learner-centred approaches. For example, the cut-off point of the majority of the students in this school is 70 out 250 marks. So you can imagine how difficult it is to deal with them. . . . "[40] The words of the Academic Mistress above indicate that despite the language of instruction obstacle, the low quality of students selected to join community secondary schools in Tanzania worsens the academic performance of these schools.

Following the above observations, Thungu, Wandera, Gachie, and Alumande clearly show the importance of reading when they say that "where there is little reading, therefore, there will be little learning".[41] According to them, by reading the learner acquires the speed and the required skills. This notion is quite agreeable because if a student is not able to read English, it becomes extremely difficult for him or her to understand what is written in every subject and will, therefore, perform poorly in all subjects. In regard to reading English, we are of the opinion that reading is an integral part of the process of learning. Provided that English continues to be the LoI, teachers, the government, and parents have to make sure that students are able to read English. If every stakeholder commits oneself to helping students to be able to read the language; it is our belief that there will be a drastic change in both reading and comprehending what is being read, and eventually to academic performance in examinations.

Students' Ability to Speak English Language

The second aspect is the students' ability to listen and speak English language. Here our intention was to determine whether students in community secondary schools could speak English. The results are indicated in the table below.

---

40. Makunja, "Challenges facing Teachers," 33.

41. Thungu, Wandera, Gachie, and Alumande, *Mastering PTE Education*, 32; cf. Kinyaduka & Kiwara, "Language of Instruction," 93.

Table 14: Ability to Speak English

	Speaking English			
Responses	Frequency	Percent	Percent	Cumulative Percent
Very Good	2	2.5	2.5	2.5
Good	35	43.8	43.8	46.3
Poor	38	47.5	47.5	93.8
Bad	5	6.3	6.3	100
Total	80	100	100	

Source: *Field Work, September,* 2016

As one can note, table 14 above shows the ability of students in community secondary schools to speak English. The result is that 38 (47.5%) respondents were poor in speaking English, 35 (43.8%) respondents were good at speaking English, while 2 (2.5%) respondents could speak it very well. Moreover, 5 (6.3%) of the respondents said that they were bad at speaking English. Similar results were obtained by Vuzo's research among form one students in one of the government secondary schools in Tanzania. Vuzo found that when students were asked questions in class, they did not respond. They just kept silent because of their inability to speak English. One of the students interviewed by Vuzo related thus: "*Wanafunzi wengine huomba kujieleza kwa Kiswahili. Mwalimu akikataa basi watanyamaza kimya . . .* Some students ask for the permission to express themselves in Kiswahili. If the teacher refuses, they remain silent."[42] Here, it is vivid that speaking is an integral part of listening; although one person initiates, both speaker and listener are constantly changing roles to form an interaction of a teacher and a student in the learning process. Hence, speaking fluent English to both students and teachers is very important for learning purposes. It was noted in our study that most students who could properly write English could also read, speak and understand the language and vice versa.

Thungu, Wandera, Gachie, and Alumande are of the view that speaking and listening are a kind of interaction (listen-respond-listen) which learners find difficulties with; and thus, it suggests that they "need special attention during the teaching of oral skills."[43] We agree with Thungu, Wan-

---

42. Vuzo, "Stakeholders' Opinions," 137.
43. Thungu, Wandera, Gachie, and Alumande, *Mastering PTE Education,* 2.

dera, Gachie and Alumande. They observed that speaking and listening of English should both be given an utmost attention because it is true that the two go together. If students are not able to listen to English properly, it will be obvious that they will also not be able to speak the language which they cannot listen. Undoubtedly, if students are not able to listen to English that means they even do not know the English words; and hence, they cannot write, read, or understand it.

Students' Ability to Listen and Understand English Language

The third aspect which concerns English proficiency is listening and understanding the language. Listening and understanding is part and parcel of the learning process simply because when the teacher teaches, students must sit down to listen. If they cannot listen to the language then it becomes a big problem as they will not understand what is being taught. The table below shows responses from the field in regard to aspects of listening and understanding English.

Table 15: Ability to listen and Understand English

Understanding English				
Responses	Frequency	Percent	Percent	Cumulative Percent
Very Good	2	2.5	2.5	2.5
Good	36	45	45	47.5
Poor	36	45	45	92.5
Bad	6	7.5	7.5	100
Total	80	100	100	

Source: *Field Work, September, 2016*

Table 15 above shows the ability of students in community secondary schools to understand English as used in teaching. In this table, the results were that 45% of the respondents said they were poor in understanding English, and 45% said were good at understanding English. In addition, 2.5% declared that they understood the language very well. Similar results were obtained in a qualitative research conducted by Ndalichako and Komba in some community secondary schools in Tanzania. In their research, one student confessed to hate Mathematics subject due to poor English background: The student said: "I hate Mathematics because I do not understand it. The teacher uses English in teaching and wants us to ask questions in English while we are not conversant with that language because of our poor foundation of English language when we were in Primary school. . . . "[44] Ndalichako and Komba's research indicates that the English language taught at primary schools, which is not spoken in everyday life, does not provide pupils sufficient vocabulary to grasp the taught content in secondary schools.

From our above presented data, it was clear that many people (45%) were poor in understanding English. It is still obvious that if students are not able to understand the language of instruction, it will definitely contribute to their poor academic performance as most of them will not understand what is being taught in the class. Following the above results, we are of the opinion that teachers should work hard so as to help students be able to listen and understand English because if this is not achieved, many students will continue performing poorly at their Form Four examinations. Students are also advised to take personal initiatives to learn the English language if the policy-makers still hold on English as being the country's language of instruction in secondary schools.

Fisher and Frey emphasize on the importance of understanding what is being taught in the classroom in order to enhance good performance in examinations. Fisher says that students sometimes feel that they have understood while they have not; and if you do not check on them, they will remain with this situation. The situation will be evident when they are given a test or examination. Here is when they become aware that they did not understand. For committed teachers, checking for understanding is a systematic and continuous process; and it is this style which will lead to effectiveness in the learning process.[45]

We agree with Fisher and Frey's assertion that understanding English is very important and that checking if students really understand is also an important parameter in the learning process. The reason is that, under normal circumstances, there is no learning without listening because a student will listen, understand, write and speak the language. The four parameters are interrelated in order to make the learning process effective.

44. Ndalichako & Komba, "Students' Subject Choice," 54.
45. Fisher & Frey, *Checking for Understanding*.

In addition, Gathumbi and Masembe declare that " . . . poor listening (and understanding) often affects nervousness, which is in turn detrimental to one's ability to respond."[46] It is quite true that poor understanding and listening affects the learning process. It makes students dull and with inadequate critical stance.[47] Moreover, if students are able to listen and understand English, it will promote their performance in class. Hence, one can see that, given its importance, listening and understanding are emphasized even by other scholars in the educational sector, and even in all other sectors. Listening is of prime importance in teaching and learning process. Therefore, a good listening enhances a good writing because as students advance to higher levels, they are required to listen to the teachers' teachings and write their own notes from their understanding of what they listen and read.

Students' Ability to Write English

The fourth aspect was to know whether students were able to write English or not. The results are recorded in the table below.

Table 16: Ability to Write English

Writing English				
Responses	Frequency	Percent	Percent	Cumulative Percent
Very Good	2	2.5	2.5	2.5
Good	36	45	45	47.5
Poor	37	46.3	46.3	93.8
Bad	5	6.3	6.3	100
Total	80	100	100	

Source: *Field Work, September, 2016*

Table 16 above presents the data of students and their ability to write English which have either positive or negative impact on their performance. According to the table above, 46.3% declared that they were poor in writing English, 45% were good, 6.3% were bad, and 2.5% could write very well. Following the data above, it is evident that most (45%) and (6.3%) students

46. Gathumbi & Masembe, *Principles and Techniques*, 4.
47. Qorro, "Matatizo ya Kutumia Kiingereza," 24–30.

could not write English properly. This was an obvious contribution to their failure at Form Four as they could not communicate in papers what they knew. Writing, for students, is communication with whoever will mark their papers; it is demonstrating to those who mark their examination scripts what has been imparted in them.

Similar results of students' inability to write English were obtained by Makunja in her qualitative research on the challenges facing community secondary schools in implementing the Competence-Based Curriculum in Tanzania. In an interview session, one of the heads of schools said: "I don't know what is wrong with our government . . . they don't take education seriously. We receive students with very low ability to the extent that some of them do not even know how to read and write properly. Last year, we gave Form Ones a simple test. To our surprise, some students hardly knew how to write their names properly. Now tell me how a teacher can use CBC approaches to assist such students to understand concepts?"[48]

Another similar result was obtained by Brock-Utne and Desai. A research by Brock-Utne and Desai focused on students' ability to write using their languages of instruction in both Tanzania and South Africa. In Tanzania, Kiswahili and English were compared; and in South Africa isXhosa and English were compared. Cartoons were provided to students who were instructed to write stories on those cartoons in English and in Kiswahili (for Tanzanian students), and in English and in isXhosa (for South African students). The results, for Tanzanian students were that students (especially form ones) were able to write good stories, grammatically well-understood, in Kiswahili language as compared to English.[49]

Following the above findings, Kellough indicates the importance of assessing what students write. He contends that if teachers do not do so, most students will end up not being able to write a sentence in English because, after all, the language is very new to them. Therefore, from the data presented and discussed above, many students are not able to write English properly in secondary schools, and community secondary schools in particular. It is for this reason that poor performance at Form Four examinations will not be avoided because these students fail to communicate properly in papers what they learnt in classes.[50]

48. Makunja, "Challenges facing Teachers," 33.
49. Brock-Utne & Desai, "Expressing Oneself," 19–30.
50. Kellough, *Surviving Your First Year of Teaching*.

In addition, Thungu, Wandera, Gachie, and Alumande point out that writing is a deliberate and conscious process of forming letters on paper or other surface to record ideas that characters and words express or communicate the ideas by visible signs. According to them, "Writing skills are most difficult to master."[51] Students can, for example, achieve a high degree of correctness in spoken English, yet have difficulties in writing it. In our opinion, there is no learning without writing as there is no teaching without writing. So, the ability of students to write English is an important aspect for students' learning. If students are not able to write English properly, it will not be possible for them to succeed in the learning process. As stated above, students will unquestionably fail in their examinations because writing is recording what is understood from what the teacher taught; and it also means responding to the assignment, test, or examination provided by the teacher to test students' understanding of the subject.

STUDENTS' INABILITY TO USE ENGLISH AS THEIR LANGUAGE OF LEARNING

Having presented and discussed the data in regard to various aspects of students' use of English language in their teaching and learning process (reading, writing, speaking and understanding), the question remains: Why are students not able to master English language as a language of instruction in their study process? Under this section, we discuss the reasons for students' inability in English language as obtained from students' and teachers' open-ended questionnaires, and in the semi-structured interviews with the district officials. Hence, at the end of this sub-topic, the reader should be aware of the reasons contributing to students' inability in English in community secondary schools.

Teachers and students who were given questionnaires in the sampled schools suggested various reasons which make students in community secondary schools be unable to read, write, understand and speak English. The first reason given by teachers was the lack of learning materials, which most teachers saw it as a contributing factor for students' inability in English. Teachers in these schools contended that for effective learning and teaching, there should be enough materials which generally facilitate the teaching and learning process. This means that for students to improve

---

51. Thungu, Wandera, Gachie, and Alumande, *Mastering PTE Education*, 52.

English as a Language of Teaching and Learning

their English, and even perform better in their studies, learning and teaching materials are very crucial.

The second reason which was put forth by students is that students lack oral English practice. They said that some students feel shy to speak English and hence continue being not able to speak English, especially in front of people who seem to know more than them. The best solution to speaking English is to avoid being shy. In our opinion, there is no way that students can learn English without speaking the language. Therefore, teachers and parents have to find appropriate motivations to students to avoid being afraid of speaking the language.

In the interview with district Officials, one of them said: "*Tatizo la wanafunzi wetu kushindwa kuzungumza Kiingereza linatokana na aibu yao kuchukua hatua ya kuongea.*" [Literally means: The problem of our students to fail to speak English is a result of their failure to try to *speak* the language.].[52] It is possible that the District Official's statement sounds quite true, and that it is necessary for students to stop being shy to speak the language. The problem here is the origin of the shame. Why do they feel shameful speaking the language?

We can respond to the above question by asserting that shamefulness emerges from their self-awareness of doing mistakes as grown up people. Students themselves stated this in Vuzo's research among form one students: "*Tunatumia mchanganyiko . . . tunaogopa kuchekwa tukikosea English. . . .* We use both English and Kiswahili because we are scared of being laughed at when we make mistakes in English."[53] Any language is better learned by people during early childhood than during adulthood. Language learners take longer times to learn a new language during adulthood than during childhood. This is what most likely happens to students' transition from Kiswahili, learned from childhood and used for more than seven years at school, to English, a foreign language lightly learned in primary schools and not spoken in normal daily interactions. This is what we stated in the statement of the problem in chapter one above. We would affirm, therefore, that practice is the only thing to make shameful students perfect in their English should the policy-makers continue to emphasize on English as a language of instruction for secondary schools in Tanzania.

---

52. District official A, Personal Interview, September, 2016.

53. Vuzo, "Stakeholders' Opinions," 135, for examples of how both Kiswahili and English are used, please see Kadeghe, "Code-Switching in Tanzanian Classrooms," 118–122.

It is well known that if one would like to excel in anything, practice is very central to the success. For English, which is a third language to most Tanzanians and a language that is not used in everyday communications, to be somehow mastered, it is very crucial that practice be done in every possible aspect. This was also cemented by teachers in their responses that having students from the same locality brings many problems because they mix more than three languages (English, Kiswahili, and their vernaculars) in their academic discussions. Moreover, Snow, when discussing the basic principles of language learning stated the importance of *practice* for the mastery of the language. We agree that the learning of any kind, including the learning of English language, becomes effective if it is accompanied with practice. That is why, most subjects particularly those of science require practical exercises after doing a theory. There is also a saying that "practice makes perfect" which really emphasizes on the importance of practicing what a student has learnt. It is for this reason that we encourage the importance of *practicing* English in writing, reading, listening and more importantly speaking the language if a proper use of the language in teaching and learning is to fully be realized.[54]

What we see is that there is no simple language which can be mastered simply. Effort is required in order to read, write, understand and speak the language fluently. Marzano et al. clearly see practice as a very crucial aspect for learning when they say: "homework and practice are instructional techniques that are well known to teachers. Both provide students with opportunities to deepen their understanding and skills relative to content that has been initially presented to them."[55] So, as Marzano et al. have said, and as our data from the field clearly indicate, practice should not be avoided if students have to properly learn the English language to help them improve their performance.

In addition, poor language (English) background is the third reason for students' inability in English. Most students have very poor English background. It is very unfortunate that they join community secondary schools with very little understanding of the language which at secondary schools becomes a medium of instruction. So, from a point where they have very little knowledge, they are now supposed to use the language in every subject; and hence, because of the poor background they fail in everything. It is such a situation which prompts us to hold the opinion that Kiswahili,

---

54. Snow, *From Language Learners to Language Teachers*, 22.
55. Marzano, et al. *Classroom Instruction*, 60.

the native language and the language spoken everywhere by both students and teachers, should be favored as the language of instruction.

A similar result was obtained by Mwipopo's research. In his qualitative research done in one of the Tanzanian schools, Mwipopo quoted a student confessing that English was the main cause for students' failures in examinations. The student stated: "At the end of the day, they end up failing. It is just that English was not our medium of communication in primary school. And now in secondary school they're supposed to know, to learn all these vocabularies that are new. It was a challenge."[56] The words of this student indicate that most students who are academically smart in primary schools where Kiswahili is the language of instruction fail to perform in secondary schools when the language changes to English. This change is both abrupt and fascinating to them. Students face two tasks at a time: to learn the vocabularies of the taught subjects, and to learn the content of those subjects, which is so challenging to the beginner of secondary school education who did not had a proper foundation of that language before.

The point of poor English foundation was repeatedly mentioned by teachers in the questionnaires and educational officials who were interviewed. Moreover, as said above, English is a third language to most Tanzanians. The first language is the mother tongue followed by the national language, which is Kiswahili. So, in this situation students learn both Kiswahili and English; and unfortunately, English is not widely used as a spoken language in Tanzania. Consequently, students put more efforts on Kiswahili which is widely used and the language they use in their everyday communications almost everywhere.

The fourth reason for students' inability in using English is the shortage of English teachers in the country. It is very unbecoming that we have a language which is very useful and is a new one; however, it has very few teachers to teach it. It is also unfortunate that in community secondary schools one can find some students going without an English teacher. Most of the teachers for the English language are in government and privately operated secondary schools which have good payments to their teachers.

The reason for having few English teachers is that many people are afraid of studying the language right from primary schools. The problem is exacerbated by fear of people to study the language; consequently, we have a few teachers both in primary and secondary schools who dare to

---

56. Mwipopo, "Secondary School Graduates' Personal Experiences," 142, cf. Nomlomo & Vuzo, "Language Transition," 76–78.

study it. In addition, the available teachers are also taken by private schools which have better salaries and more fringe benefits as compared to the government and community secondary schools. Hence, under this situation, the government has an obligation to encourage many students who go for teachers' collages to study English as a teaching subject; however, efforts to find good English teachers who are native English speakers have to start right from primary schools to higher levels of education.

The fifth reason, students mentioned that excessive use of vernacular languages was another factor which makes students unable in English. Most primary schools have pupils from the same locality, people who share their background and language. This means that when they are at school they most often use local languages in their interactions. This is also a trend for community secondary schools, which unlike the government owned secondary schools, have students from the same localities. These also use either their local language or Kiswahili in their normal conversations. However, in order to enforce the use of English, there are some punitive measures imposed for those who are found talking Kiswahili or vernacular languages. Unfortunately, these measures have not yielded the best anticipated results. This is also supported by Jackson when discussing the way culture affects learning among the African Americans.[57] It is true that one's culture has effects on the language, and vice versa. Deliberate efforts have to be put in place to ensure English is more used than vernacular languages. This is because, as also teachers contended, punishment has not helped to stop students from using their local languages in their normal communications when are at school. The question here is whether it can be possible to stop students from using their vernaculars which they have studied and internalized them from their childhood to force them to English, a foreign language imposed to them at their grown up age in secondary schools.

Negative attitude towards English was the sixth reason which contributes to students' inability in English. Most students have developed an attitude that English is a difficulty language; consequently, they do not put any effort to study it because they are despaired. Hence, all stakeholders have to make sure that efforts are put in order to eradicate this attitude among students. Otherwise, if this continues, we will continue having students who are poor in English and unable to do well in their studies. The question here is whether it is possible to eradicate this attitude which students have internalized for years.

57. Jackson, *African American Education*.

English as a Language of Teaching and Learning

In learning, just like in other areas, if people believe something to be difficult and feel that they are unable to do it, they will never do it efficiently. In short, most students admitted that they hated English language for the reason that it was the language they met on the way. It was not the language they started with it in primary school, and neither was it the language they used in normal life communications. Students and teachers said that lack of teachers' and students' motivation was the seventh factor which made students fail in English and hence fail even in other subjects. Both teachers and students must be motivated in order for them to do better and better. Students should be motivated by both teachers and parents in case they perform well in English. Moreover, students should be promised rewards if they perform well in English; this will probably make them increase their efforts in the subject. So, if the Tanzanian government seriously wants to improve the status of English in the country it has to motivate both teachers and students. On the one hand, teachers have to be motivated so that they themselves struggle towards knowing English and then working hard to teach students. On the other hand students have to be motivated so that they may work hard in studying the English language; and those who perform well should be rewarded by teachers, parents, and even the government.

In the eighth reason, it was also disclosed that students' inability in English was contributed by the fact that English was only spoken and learnt at schools, and specifically in classrooms. When students went home, where they took a considerable time of the day, they used Kiswahili and vernacular languages. If English was spoken at homes, it could consolidate their learning of the language. Therefore, following this reason, English was just a forced language. It was not the language which teachers and students were comfortable with it. They suggested that parents who are good at speaking English are encouraged to speak the language at homes so that students may continue learning the language even at homes. In addition, parents should take initiatives of providing English tuitions for their children, in whatever means possible, so as to help them improve their language proficiency.[58] The question here is whether parents at homes may have the ability to teach their children a better English than the teachers at the students' respective schools, if not causing confusions.

In their ninth reason, students also maintained that even teachers used Kiswahili most of their time in the classrooms when teaching. They

---

58. Mlay, "The Influence of the Language of Instruction," 13.

also used English only when in the school surroundings, especially when they interacted with students not often among teachers. This also impaired the learning of English. In the efforts to use English in teaching secondary education and above, it is quite unfortunate that even English teachers use Kiswahili in teaching the subject against the requirement of the curricular. It would be worthwhile for all teachers, those teaching English and other subjects, to use English in teaching students who now struggle to learn English. This means that they have to respect and remain faithful to the requirement of the curricular. By teachers using Kiswahili, they deprive students the opportunity to learn new vocabularies and pronunciation, if not jeopardizing the reputation of English language which boasts reputation all over the world.

STUDENTS' POOR PERFORMANCE IN FORM FOUR EXAMINATIONS

In the previous section, we discussed the reasons that make students unable to master English as a language of teaching and learning. In this section, we discuss the reasons that contribute to students' failure at Form Four examinations as provided by students' and teachers' questionnaires and in the interview with the district officials. There were various reasons stipulated as factors for students' failure at Form Four examinations in community secondary schools. The first reason mentioned was truancy of students from attending studies at schools. It was said that most students in community secondary schools did not attend classes regularly; and hence, this affected their performance. Chaube and Chaube view truancy as one of the causes for students' poor academic performance when they say that "some student run away from the school. This may be due to disinterestedness in studies."[59] They argue that the tendency has a negative impact on educational achievement. Consequently, both teachers and parents should work together to ensure that students do not miss classes because it will affect their performance in future. However, the question is about the reasons for students who were faithful attendants and passed well at primary schools practice truancy when at secondary schools. Most likely, their inability to understand the taught content can be the possible reason. Students find no necessity to waste time for things they do not understand.

---

59. Chaube and Chaube, *School Organization*, 134.

The second reason mentioned was family conflicts. Students in the schools visited saw family conflicts as being a very big problem since in a situation where there were conflicts, students were affected psychologically and were not properly assisted in their studies. It is for this reason that parents have to know that conflicts in the families have negative effects on students' performance.

It was also realized that some students had examination fevers in the normal school formative assessments; consequently, they failed to concentrate and perform better at Form Four summative examinations. Some students were very fearful to examinations; this alone made them not be able to perform the way they were supposed to perform. Coombs speaks about becoming nervous as a result of failure of some students in the examinations. Coombs has the opinion that becoming nervous and examination fevers are students' frequent occasions that greatly contribute to students' failures. These aspects can be controlled by the introduction of counseling departments in each secondary school to deal with these and similar issues facing students.[60]

Family poverty was mentioned as the third reason for massive failures of students at form four summative examinations because the families did not support them, not because they did not like, but because they had no money to do so. In fact, there are still families which cannot help their children in terms of the basic educational requirements. The families are not able to provide adequate nutrition to their children, which is also very important for their brain development. When they are grown up the ones who had inadequate food to eat at home can hardly be expected to perform better. This assertion is also confirmed by Jackson when she maintained that "a basic link exists between poverty and learning."[61] She further asserted that low-income communities mean underfunded schools and children which lead these children into poor performance. Hence, teachers are advised to give more examinations and tests to students so that they are accustomed to examinations leading them into reduced fear for examinations.[62]

On top of that, the fourth reason is that most of the students in community secondary schools used their time playing instead of studying. This practice impeded their ability to perform at Form Four summative examinations. Toft and Mancina emphasize the importance of appropriate use of time

60. Coombs, *Successful Teaching*.
61. Jackson, *African American Education*, 73.
62. Ibid.

for students with their limited time of being at school when they say that "time is an equal opportunity resource. All of us, regardless of gender, race, creed or national origin, have exactly the same number of hours in a week. No matter how famous we are, no matter how rich or poor, we get 168 hours to spend each week-no more, no less."[63] Their emphasis here is that students as well as other people should use this nonrenewable resource wisely.

Moreover, Arends speaks about the engaged time for students learning when he says that "the amount of time students actually spend on an activity or task . . ."[64] We find the arguments of the above scholars, Toft and Mancina and Arends, who are concerned with proper use of time for students' academic performance to be very informative. Students as well as their teachers are advised to use time wisely as well. However, the question is not the use of much time, but of understanding what is studied. Therefore, the question of proper use of time should go together with that of understanding what is being studied.

In line with the fourth reason above, the fifth reason was that students lacked adequate preparations in order to pass their form four examinations. Preparations had to start from form one through form four. As one might be aware, passing at form four examinations involves cumulative studied materials from form one to form four. So, students should be seriously studying right from form one to form four in order to pass the form four summative examinations. Therefore, all education stakeholders should encourage and train students to use this important and nonrenewable resource wisely. However, the problem with this advice is the way they can use their time studying a thing they hardly understand due to language barrier as was revealed in the data discussed above.

TOWARDS IMPROVING THE USE OF ENGLISH AS LANGUAGE OF TEACHING AND LEARNING

What have students and teachers to say about the best way to improve English proficiency in community secondary schools and the performance in general? After discussing the reasons for the lack of English proficiency in the previous section, this subsection discusses some recommendations on what should be done to improve English language if the government and other stakeholders would prefer to continue using it as a language of

---

63. Toft & Mancina, *Becoming a Master Student*, 61.
64. Arends, *Learning to Teach*, 40.

instruction. The recommendations were received from students' and teachers' questionnaires and in the interviews with the district officials. When asked about what should be done to improve English to students in community secondary schools, both teachers and students had the following suggestions: first, all were of the opinion that the government should increase English learning materials to enable students have an opportunity and access to these materials which will eventually enhance their ability in English language. Their recommendation was based on the fact that learning materials were very few as compared to students they received annually.

Second, both teachers and students said that debate gatherings in schools and between schools should be encouraged since it will help students to learn how to compose English sentences and speak them in front of other people. This will also help students to develop self-confidence and remove shamefulness, which is very much required if students have to speak good English. According to Gathumbi and Masembe, debate competitions will also facilitate students to learn English in all its areas: meaning, reading, writing, understanding, and speaking.[65] Moreover, Aggarwal shows the importance of debates and he calls debate as " . . . an intellectual programme in which two or more students holding opposite views on a particular topic present arguments."[66] The two scholars above have indicated the importance of debates for language improvements which should be emphasized in schools for both students and teachers to participate.

However, it should be remembered that debates are currently not given priority, particularly in community secondary schools. As stated above, debates are of prime importance for language development. In order to improve English, teachers maintained that those who are teaching the language must be motivated so that they may gain more momentum in helping students. Currently, English teachers, in line with other teachers, are very de-motivated because there is nothing more they gain other than their monthly salaries which even those who teach other subjects also obtain. Hence, it will be worthwhile if the government motivates them even by giving just a token prize; English teachers will feel recognized and, therefore, work very hard.

Third, both teachers and students advised that it should be compulsory for both students and teachers to speak English at schools. This statement means that code switching and code mixing should be discouraged to a great extent. This, according to them, will help students practice speaking

---

65. Gathumbi and Masembe, *Principles and Techniques*.
66. Aggarwal, *Principles, Methods and Techniques*, 105.

the language if they want any service or help from teachers. Currently, all conversations between teachers and students, and between students themselves, are mostly made in Kiswahili. Hence, since schools are academic areas, and it is obligatory that English is the language of instruction, the government should emphasize and administer to ensure that every person speaks English. Both teachers and students are required to speak English so as to improve their language proficiency.

Fourth, another suggestion made by students is that teachers should avoid code switching and code mixing while teaching in the classrooms. As stated above, code switching and code mixing practices affect students' learning as for teachers doing so, students miss the opportunity to listen and learn the proper English vocabularies and correct sentences. In this regard, the Ministry of Education should ensure that principles of education to students are adhered, one of which concerns the language of instruction.

As stated above, most of the time, teachers use Kiswahili in classrooms thinking that they emphasize for students to understand; they do not know that this practice hampers students' understanding of English. Following this code switching of teachers from English to Kiswahili, some students and teachers advised that the government should see the possibility of either making English a medium of instruction at primary schools or making Kiswahili a medium of instruction at secondary schools. Making English a medium of instruction at primary schools will help students to have a good language foundation which will eventually be helpful at providing secondary education.

Also by making Kiswahili a medium of instruction at secondary education, it will help students who are now conversant with Kiswahili to continue enjoying the use of the language which they are conversant in the teaching and learning process. The problem, as stated in the statement of the problem in the introductory chapter of this book, has been the dramatic shift from the use of Kiswahili at most primary schools to solely using English at secondary schools. This dramatic shift makes the student concentrate on language struggle instead of struggling with the contents of taught subject matters. Most students in this study affirmed that in the early years of their secondary studies (forms one and two) the language struggle becomes too big to clearly understand what is being taught by teachers. Most of them develop creaming capacities in order to answer questions provided by their teachers in tests and examinations. Here the government should make a deliberate decision on the language of instruction to

English as a Language of Teaching and Learning

use—Kiswahili or English. However, reaching at this decision, there should be thorough discussions by education stakeholders. It should not be a one person's decision like the Minister for education, as it once happened in the past years when the Minister decided to abolish some subjects in secondary schools and combined some other subjects. Despite the above suggestion, it is our opinion that any attempts to make English as LoI in Tanzania from primary schools to University will hardly be a better option because it will be selling our cultural identity to the foreign imperial language.

The fifth suggestion disclosed by teachers was to encourage essay writing competitions for students. It was disclosed that this practice was disappearing in most parts of the country, especially in community secondary schools. It was acknowledged that competitions should have rewards, for instance, for the top ten runners. Here, the government, the private sector, or individual people can fund the competitions. The competitions may be at different levels such as at a school, ward, division, district, region and national levels depending on the funding. Hence, essay writing competitions will more likely improve writing skills for students in community secondary schools. The problem with this suggestion is based on the lack of English competent teachers to encourage the writing of such essays. Since English is a problem from primary to higher levels, any endeavor to promote it will face this obstacle because the writing of such essays will be supervised by incompetent teachers.

Sixth, some teachers suggested that everybody should discourage the use of Kiswahili and vernacular languages at schools. According to them, the use of these languages has greatly affected the improvement of English to students in community secondary schools. Teachers should seriously prohibit the use of local languages and should also make sure that they are also part and parcel of this by-law. They insisted that students in secondary schools should avoid using Kiswahili while at schools. Since Kiswahili is taught as a subject, and English is not spoken at homes and in communities, students fail to practice and master it favoring Kiswahili. Teachers in the research area advised that teachers and students should strictly use English and ensure that those who speak Kiswahilli at schools stern measures are taken upon them. The problem that remains with their suggestion is that English is not learned from childhood. It is not the language which parents impart to their children, and neither is it the language internalized by children as they grow up; which can make them hard to abandon Kiswahili in whatever adopted strategy.

Seventh, teachers suggested that both teachers and parents should make sure that they motivate students who perform well in English. Teachers can use different ways of motivating them whereas parents can also do it to their children who seem to do well in English. If it is done properly, this will not only motivate students who are doing well, but also those who have not performed well so that they do well in future.[67] The importance of parent and guardian involvement is also confirmed by Kellough as he said "when parents (or guardians) are involved in their child's school and school work, students learn better and earn better grades and teachers experience more positive feelings about teaching."[68] It is for this reason that teachers in some schools communicate with parents and guardians by telephones, letters, e-mails or inviting the parent for short meetings when a student has shown a sudden turn for either the worse or the better in academic achievement, or in a classroom behavior. Kronowitz speaks about working with parents for efficient and effective learning. The scholar is convinced about the importance of parents to know everything about their children. He writes: Parents "have the right to be informed about their child's progress–both strengths and weaknesses."[69]

Eighth, teachers were of the opinion that in order for students to improve their language, English teachers should give as many assignments to students as possible so that when they are busy responding to the assignments they will be learning and improving their language. Students also mentioned this point by saying that teachers should give them many home works and assignments as possible to enable them discuss in groups and write in papers.[70]

Chaube and Chaube are in favor of giving many home works and mentioned assignments like weekly and monthly tests on top of other assignments. They feel that the assignment will help students do better in their examinations. Therefore, when students do assignments they practice what they learnt in classes and this will likely improve their English.[71]

---

67. Tileston, *What every Teacher should Know*.

68. Kellough, *Surviving Your First Year of Teaching*, 63.

69. Kronowitz, *Beyond Student Teaching*, 102.

70. For more insights on how the teacher can motivate students towards improving their reading, writing, and speaking the English language, please see Thomas & Robinson, *Improving Reading*.

71. Chaube & Chaube, *School Organization*.

English as a Language of Teaching and Learning

Ninth, students claimed that the government should also make sure that they recruit competent English teachers. In their views, some English teachers seem to be not competent in English and hence cannot help students to improve their language. If English teachers are competent, they will be able to meet the reasons for teaching which includes making a contribution to society, enjoying freedom to work with few constraints, transmitting academic content, helping students develop as individuals, and being rewarded for good performance.[72] It is obvious, therefore, that teachers with poor English proficiency will produce poor students in English.

However, the above suggestions by teachers and students leave us with some tangible risks to contemplate as we consider for the language of instruction and academic performance issue in Tanzanian secondary schools, and even colleges and universities. Kimizi lists the risks that will be incurred if English continues to be a language of instruction in secondary schools and higher-learning institutions:

> The general implications from the continued use of English as the medium of [teaching and] learning at secondary and higher education levels result into a number of high cost disadvantages. These include cramming and parroting on the part of students doing examinations and lack of cognitive understanding of concepts introduced in the lessons; poor student participation in the learning process and total lack of student-teacher interaction on account of inadequate fluency in English as a LOI and such students fail to take a critical stance on ideas presented in lectures and readings; uncritical and undigested presentation of concepts by teachers whose proficiency levels in English as a LOI is low. Teachers sometimes use their college notes to teach secondary school students after having [themselves] failed to digest them; and equating access to English as a language to automatic access to scientific and technological knowledge.[73]

The above quotation indicates that the teachers' and students' suggestions are inadequate to enhance a proper masterly of what students learn using a foreign language. It also entails that Tanzanian policy-makers have to clearly distinguish between English as a language to be used for communication and as a language to be used for teaching and learning knowledge.

For English to be used as a language for teaching and learning knowledge, both teachers and students should be able to listen and understand,

---

72. Savage, Savage & Amstrong, *Teaching in the Secondary School*.
73. Kimizi, "Why has the Language of Instruction?" 13.

write, speak, and read it. In other words, it should be the language that governs their life in general. It should be part of their worldview. It matters very little to believe, as has been being believed, that students and teachers will learn English and become part of their cultural worldview in the course of using it, as stated by teachers and students in their suggestions above, or through sending pupils to English Medium kindergarten and primary schools. The results from our research and from other previous researches cited in this book have demonstrated that English is still a hindrance towards the proper understanding of the taught subjects in all levels of Tanzania's education system, preprimary, primary, secondary schools, colleges, and universities, despite its continuous use as a medium of instruction for many years.[74]

---

74. Cf. Qorro, "Matatizo ya Kutumia Kiingereza," 28–29; Masele, "Kiswahili au Kiingereza?" 31–33; Kalmanlehto, "Mixed Domains," 50–66.

Chapter 5

Conclusion

"Education should be treated as a strategic agent for mind-set transformation and for the creation of a well-educated nation, sufficiently equipped with the knowledge needed to competently and competitively solve the development challenges which face the nation."

—URT, The Tanzanian Development Vision, 19.

The major endeavor of any educational policy, in any country is to ensure the provision of *quality Education* to its citizens in all levels of its educational system. This is also what applies to Tanzania and its educational policy. The Tanzanian educational policy clearly states: "Education should be treated as a strategic agent for mind-set transformation and for the creation of a well-educated nation, sufficiently equipped with the knowledge needed to competently and competitively solve the development challenges which face the nation. In this light, the education system should be restructured and transformed qualitatively with a focus on promoting creativity and problem solving."[1] Following this policy statement, and as we have discussed in this book,

> quality education is that which is capable of bringing about *change* in our learners—change from less knowledgeable to more knowledgeable individuals, from less confident to more confident individuals, from dependent to independent individuals, from

1. URT, *The Tanzanian Development Vision*, 19.

job seekers to job creators, and so on. We can achieve this change by making a concerted effort to have education that encourages learners to take an active part in the learning process, by insisting that education should allow and actually foster creative learning and creative thinking, and that it gives learners the responsibility to construct and generate knowledge through discussion rather than through transmission and rote learning."[2]

The question is whether the URT and Qorro's lucid suggestions above can be attainable in a current Tanzanian situation where students hardly understand what they learn due to the language of instruction used.

The main concern of this book was to examine the use of English as a language of instruction in community secondary schools in the Tanzanian context. It examined the relationship between the use of English, a foreign language, poorly understood by both teachers and students, and the quality of education obtained by the use of this language in teaching and learning at secondary school levels. The research was specifically done in Mbeya District Council using both quantitative and qualitative approaches. The main hypothesis that guided the study was *"poor performance in form four summative examinations in community secondary schools is caused by the low proficiency of English of students and teachers who teach them."*

It has been vivid in this study that, by the use of English as a language of teaching and learning, students in community secondary schools in the study area attain poor performance in form four summative examinations, which is also caused by the poor English language proficiency to both teachers and students.[3] The problem of students' failures at form four has to be checked with seriousness since it leads to a number of other problems resulting from ignorance. It is also a fact that students have to receive this important right of being educated, which will enlighten them in various areas of their life.

On the basis of data obtained from the field, it is indicated that students' failures is a dramatic problem in Mbeya District Council selected as representative of the majority District councils in Tanzania. It was noted, however, that there were several reasons which contributed to students'

2. Qorro, "Does Lnguage of Instruction affect Quality?" 9.

3. For a similar conclusion on this issue in other places of Tanzania and the world, please see Feast, "The Impact of IELTS Scores"; Fakeye & Ogunsuji, "English Language Proficiency"; Komba, et al., "Comparison between Students' Academic Performance"; Qorro, "A Qualitative Study on Teaching"; Maleki and Zangani, "A Survey on the Relationship"; and Kinyaduka & Kiwara, "Language of Instruction."

failure at form four examinations: truancy of students, family conflicts, examination fevers and the fear for examinations. In addition, family poverty also contributes to students' poor performance and most students spend most of their time playing instead of reading. However, the main cause of students' failures revealed in this study is *students' and teachers' poor English background*; and that, English is the third language after vernaculars and Kiswahili which renders them to lack proficiency.

Moreover, excessive use of local languages affects the development of English, which in turn causes students' failures when it comes to using English to answer questions. Other causes include lack of motivation to both teachers and students towards the English language; and more important, the fact that English is only spoken at schools, and only when teaching in class, not outside the classroom and at homes where students and teachers spend most of their life time. All these aspects make English to remain a marginal language in the Tanzanian context.

In a nutshell, the following were some recommendations from respondents: to ensure that debates are promoted at secondary schools, to motivate both teachers and students so that they work hard, to make it compulsory for students and teachers to speak English at schools, to emphasize that teachers should avoid code switching and code mixing while teaching in the classrooms, the government to see the possibility of either making English a medium of instruction at primary schools in order to have one language used for teaching and learning from lower levels to higher ones, or make Kiswahili a medium of instruction at secondary schools in order to have a continuation of the language used at primary schools.

In addition, to encourage essay competitions for students, to discourage the use of Kiswahili and vernacular languages at schools, teachers and parents to make sure that they motivate students who perform well in English, teachers to give many assignments to students so that when they are busy can have frequent contact with the language through writing and reading, and the government to make sure that they recruit competent English teachers who will be roll model to their students. These strategies, according to teachers' and students' suggestions, could help mitigate the existing inadequate proficiency in English language among teachers and students.

However, Mbeya District Council has been just a case study; the problem for this study and the recommendations provided by students and teachers above hit many students in Tanzania, and most likely other countries of Africa and the world having similar problems in the language of instruction. It is with this understanding that we provide our recommendations in the following paragraphs.

Our first, and predominant, recommendation touches the Tanzanian government and its decision on an appropriate LoI. In the current situation where Kiswahili language is used by almost all people throughout the country, is being accepted by some countries in the East African Community (EAC), and has penetrated the entire people's cultural worldview, we strongly recommend that Tanzanian policy-makers consider changing the LoI in secondary schools and higher learning institutions from English to Kiswahili as was suggested by Jackson Makweta's Presidential Commission of 1980. This is because the abrupt change from Kiswahili to English as the primary school leaver joins secondary education does not only culturally intimidate the student beginning secondary school studies, but also provides a psychological torture that ruins the student's identity and right to knowledge. Moreover, there is an urgent need to have a correlation between the language used to educate experts for serving people in various sectors, and the language which is understood and used by service recipients. Since language is one of the major vehicles of culture, the trained expert is forced to imitate a foreign culture through the language used in imparting knowledge making him/her unfit to serve people in his/her own country.

Moreover, the government should make sure that it provides equal enrolment to all children into schools regardless of their gender, ethnic belonging, religion, place, race and even disability. There is hardly any need for creating classes of people within the free and democratic country like Tanzania. It means that the existing division between the majority users of Kiswahili as LoI (in the majority government pre-primary and primary schools) and the minority users of English (in the minority private English Medium pre-primary and primary schools) has not been a just practice. An intentional attempt towards having Kiswahili as LoI for all levels of education suggested above will greatly eradicate the growing classism and enhance solidarity and unity among people.

It is good that the government introduced community secondary schools which draw many children from their nearby areas to attend secondary education; however, this blessing required to go hand in hand with ensuring that students pass their form four summative examinations because just ending at form four is not very helpful to respective students and to the country, particularly in this twenty first century. There is a necessity for the government to at least prepare well-trained teachers in English, if it still continues with it as LoI, since it is a base of all other subjects. Here, we mean that though students have the obligation to study hard when at school, yet teachers play a great role in facilitating them. If students do not know English just because of their incompetent teachers, as in the areas assessed in this research, it will possibly be difficult for them to have better performance at any level of their study in life.

Moreover, it is hereby advised that, the government should not enroll failure students at secondary school level for joining the teaching profession. Here we mean that all students who failed in the form four and form six examinations (those with division IV) should not be taken to join teachers' colleges for the teaching profession because their poor performance is a vivid indication that they will hardly provide a significant contribution towards educational development. In regard to the current situation, Kitta and Fussy attest: "Academically weak students have flooded teacher education programmes in Tanzanian teacher colleges and universities. For example, in principle, the minimum entry qualification for the teachers' diploma programme is at least two principal passes and a subsidiary in Form Six National Examinations (ACSE). In reality, this is not always the case; students with one principal and one subsidiary are also enrolled in the programme. . . . Enrolling under-qualified candidates has far-reaching implications on the teaching and learning process."[4]

The above statement means that the poor educational performance of students joining teachers' colleges indicate that they have a low intellectual ability making it difficult to turn them into best teachers in their teacher training process. As a result, they leave the teachers' training colleges with low quality education, which will also be transmitted to students they are going to teach. Qorro clarifies this implication when she says: "the poor quality education the teacher-to-be student has received is likely to be passed on to the subsequent generation of pupils who will inevitably turn out with poorer quality of education."[5] This statement means that academically poor students joining the teaching profession make academically poor teachers, which further turns to academically poor Tanzanian generations.

The survey conducted by Hardman to review the teacher education in Tanzania revealed that "Many [students joining Teachers Training Colleges

4. Kitta and Fussy, "Bottlenecks in Preparation of Quality Teachers," 33.
5. Qorro, "Language of Instruction and Its effects," 66; cf. Sumra & Katabaro, "Declining Quality of Education," 23–24.

were] from households with low levels of parental education and non-professional livelihoods. The academic level of many of the entrants was weak and many had the minimal qualifications necessary for entrance so they were unlikely to have secure grounding in core subjects."[6] In fact, this is a clear indication that the educational sector is marginalized from the ground to the higher levels because of the poor teachers being enrolled and produced.

To emphasize on the point of the low quality of people dealing with the teaching profession, Kitta and Fussy state that the low quality of teachers is also vivid among trainers of teachers themselves. Most teacher training colleges have trainers with low or inadequate educational qualifications. Kitta and Fussy elaborate this point:

> As was the case with the quality of candidates enrolled in teacher education colleges/universities, the similar practice is with the teacher-educators/teacher trainers. For decades, teacher education colleges/universities in Tanzania have been a damping place for unqualified, under-qualified and incompetent teachers. Analysis of Basic Educational Statistics in Tanzania (BEST) for the past five years (2008—2012), revealed that teacher education colleges had employed 183 unqualified tutors both in government and non-government (URT, 2013a). Furthermore, teachers who were prepared to teach in secondary schools are assigned teaching duties in teacher education colleges. In principle, to teach in teacher education colleges, for instance, at diploma level of education, one needs to be a graduate of Bachelor of Education, as well as Masters in Education (URT, 1995). In practice, however, it has not been the case. Given shortages of graduate teachers, especially with masters' degree, diploma teacher education colleges have been run by first degree teachers of education. These teachers have qualification of Bachelor of Education (B.Ed.), Bachelor of Arts with Education (B.A.Ed.) and Bachelor of Science with Education (B.Sc. Ed.). Nevertheless, the latter graduates (B.A.Ed. and B.Sc. Ed.) were prepared to teach in secondary schools.[7]

Following the above statement, one can ask an ambiguous question: If the trainer of trainers is oneself incompetent, what should be expected to students who will be trained by trainers trained by the incompetent trainer

---

6. Hardman, "A Review of Teacher Education," 9.

7. Kitta and Fussy, "Bottlenecks in Preparation of Quality Teachers," 33; cf. Anangisye, "Developing Quality Teacher Professionals," 39.

of trainers? The above quotation indicates that the Tanzanian educational system as a whole requires a careful scrutiny to suit the current developments of the country basing on the required national and international educational standards, especially in college, secondary, and primary levels.

It should be remembered that during the colonial period, it was those who passed properly in the examinations who were taken to be teachers. This is still functional for some Universities, that those with higher Grade Point Averages (GPAs), are the ones who remain to be lecturers. It seems that something is wrong with the current educational system. Most students who join the teaching profession especially in primary schools, have divisions three and even four in their form four examinations.

At the university level, despite leaving those with higher GPAs to teach, there is also a problem on the qualification of most of those assigned to teach, in relation to the levels they teach, especially to most private Universities. Kitta and Fussy describe this problem succinctly:

> at the university level, except for Schools, Faculties, or Departments of Education, there is no teacher training for university lecturers. That is to say, all lecturers or teachers in education related academic units are and should be products of the teacher training curriculum. Unless one went through the teacher training programme, she or he cannot be offered a place to teach in the Schools, Faculties or Departments of Education at university. Indeed, according to the Tanzania Commission for Universities (TCU) regulations, a teacher graduate at least with masters degree in education should be assigned teaching duties. In reality, however, the practice is different. Teacher education universities, particularly private universities are flooded with many Tutorial Assistants (TAs) and these TAs are given courses to teach.... Tutorial Assistants (TAs) are young academics at universities who have first degree and their main duty is to supervise seminars, not to teach courses. These academicians have less qualification to teach and handle courses, until they undergo postgraduate training in their relevant fields. The practice of allocating teaching duties to even bachelor degree holders (Tutorial Assistants) to teach undergraduate classes is not only a notable violation of TCU regulations but also it undermines the efforts to prepare quality teachers. As such, student-teachers are made to receive inadequate knowledge and skills from those less pedagogically and intellectually qualified academic staff.[8]

---

8. Kitta and Fussy, "Bottlenecks in Preparation of Quality Teachers," 34.

Conclusion

In the Foreword to the *Education and Training Policy* document of 1955 by the then Tanzania's Minister of Education and Culture Professor Philemon M. Sarungi, it was stated: "A good system of education in any country must be effective on two fronts: on the *quantitative level*, to ensure access to education and equity in the distribution and allocation of resources to various segments of the society, and on the *qualitative level*, to ensure that the country produces the skills required for rapid social and economic development."[9] The minister's statement has not been effective until the recent years, especially in terms of the quality of educational outputs. Despite producing graduates who can fit in the current world of globalization, who can endeavor to deal with the prevailing national and individual problems, creators of jobs instead of being seekers of jobs, and good citizens with a high degree of patriotism, the vice versa is true. Mostly, the quality of education produced is inversely proportional to quantities of primary schools, secondary schools, colleges and universities in the country.[10] The comment on the quality of teachers in all levels described above suggests that the educational system, especially the recruiting of teachers and lecturers in Tanzanian Colleges and Universities, requires a deliberate overhauling in order to meet the minister's two above stated fronts.

In line with the above comment, the government should improve salaries for teachers in order to motivate more people to enter the teaching profession, even those whose passes are higher (especially those with Division one). We should state clearly here that low and lowly motivating salaries decrease teachers' statuses. Currently, so many people opt for teaching after all other means have failed basing on their performance.[11] Kitta and Fussy clearly elaborate this point when they say:

> A majority of the candidates admitted into teacher education programmes in Africa, Tanzania in particular are not genuinely interested in teaching as a career. . . . Teaching career is the last refuge to many students seeking employment opportunities. . . . These students take up teaching after failing to secure another job. As such, it is a common practice for teacher education colleges and universities in Africa to absorb academically weak students. Generally, these teacher trainees do not regard teaching as their chosen profession. They regard themselves being in a wrong profession, as they most craved for becoming doctors, engineers or

---

9. URT, *Education and Training Policy*, v.
10. Sumra and Rajani, "Secondary Education in Tanzania," 3.
11. Lyimo, "Analysis of Teachers' Low Payments," 5–11.

> lawyers, but their poor academic grades left them with no choice except to become teachers.... [12]

Kitta and Fussy's above statement means that though the educational sector is the wide spread profession (that all sectors have teachers), it is probably the most hated and un-respected one due to lack of adequate motivation. People do not like to join it. Even students who are still studying in secondary schools do no dream to be teachers one day after the completion of their studies. And those who have joined it dream to leave it as soon as they secure another better job than teaching.[13] We are of the opinion that if the teaching profession will be paying and motivating many young generations will be interested to join the teaching profession seriously; and those within the teaching profession will not dream to leave it to other professions which are considered to be more motivating than the teaching profession.

More specifically, the Ministry of Education and Vocational Training is also advised to ensure that there are enough and qualified teachers in community secondary schools just as are for government and private secondary schools. In Mbeya region, for example, we have several government secondary schools like Mbeya Day, Rungwe, Iyunga and Loleza secondary schools. These schools do not suffer much shortage of teachers alongside other teaching and learning materials. The issue is not for the government to allow the establishment of schools and leave them to suffer alone. More likely, the issue is to make sure that they are well-monitored in order for them to provide quality education according to the prescribed policies. The idea of having community secondary schools to enable the majority Tanzanian children acquire secondary education will be solidly implemented if these schools are well-monitored and well-nourished in terms of the quality of education they provide to them.

We also have recommendations to the mass media to take their role effectively. Mass media, both print (e.g., magazines, newspapers, and books) and electronic (e.g., videos, radios, televisions, films, and internet networks) are important in education. They can either promote or degrade education. When used in the right way, they become the nerve system towards educating society. When abused, they become the great source of disrupting society's whole worldview. This means that media have a

---

12. Kitta and Fussy, "Bottlenecks in Preparation of Quality Teachers, 32; cf. Mkumbo, "Teachers' Commitment," 224–225; Towse et al., "Non-graduate Teacher Recruitment."
13. Sumra & Katabaro, "Declining Quality of Education," 23.

Conclusion

powerful influence towards consolidating or distorting cultural values and orientations, ethical foundations, and the general human behavior.

Mugyenyi reports that ineffective use of media tarnishes people's names and dignities, or causes misunderstandings, and even wars and violence. Media can cause people to engage in unlawful acts, if used misleadingly to convey information to society, especially if people will imitate what the media portray and advocate. Issues, such as pornography, violent games, unethical music, etc., have the possibility to create aggressive behaviors to children towards their parents, teachers and fellow children. Acts, such as suicides, smoking of all kinds, and disrespect among students, and children as a whole, are most likely the results of behaviors adopted from distorted media. Therefore, media plays a great role towards education and the nurturing of society.[14]

Following the above descriptions, the mass media are obliged to play its role decently in order to enhance the use of English language in Tanzania. Media should sensitize parents and the community in general on the importance of their children to be conversant with English language for their future studies. The media should encourage parents to take special initiatives in order to help their children right at primary schools. As it is well-noted in this research, most students fail their form four examinations because of not knowing English language well, which is also a result of poor English background from primary schools. The media should also encourage parents to help students who are already at community secondary schools. This may possibly help them to pass their examinations. Consequently, given the importance of mass media and how community members value and trust them, it is, therefore, very important for them to take responsibility to help sensitize community members on the issue of education just stated.

Research by Bempechat indicate that parents also have a very considerable role to play in order to help their children perform well at form four levels, just as it is the case for all other levels, and in the cognitive growth as a whole.[15] Parents belong to particular families. It is in those families where parents exert educational influence towards their children. According to Mugyenyi, the family, whether single family (i.e., of one parent caring for the child or children), nuclear family (i.e., of two parents and child or children), or extended family (i.e., of one or more additional people apart from those

---

14. Mugyenyi, *Aspects of Sociology*, 17–19.
15. Bempechat, "The Role of Parent Involvement."

in the nuclear family) has a great role to play in the support for children's education.[16] Mugyenyi mentions the following as some of those roles:

- "Buying the required materials for learning, like textbooks, pencils, and exercise books.
- Teaching children at home by parents.
- Parents helping their children to complete the homework.
- Parents being role models for their children.
- Having materials in the hole which facilitate learning like; light, chats, newspapers, TVs, computers, wall clocks. . . .
- Provision of parental love, proper diet, all of which make the child to develop mentally.
- Provision of pocket money and school visits."[17]

Therefore, though the family consists of related members within a particular society, it has a great deal of contribution towards the educational stance of the entire society, especially the struggle towards improving their performance. This is made possible through parents' active roles towards their children.

Parents have to ensure that their children have a good foundation of English so that if they are selected to join community secondary schools, they can be better. It will not be wise for parents to leave the role of ensuring quality education to the government and teachers alone. Parents have also to make sure that their children who are already at community secondary schools participate in remedial classes both for English and other subjects. Parents have to love and motivate their children to learn English by rewarding them when they pass, or promising to reward them if they will pass the examinations. Indeed, parents have the role of ensuring that their children have good English foundation so that they do not stumble in their studies in future.[18] "To love one's children," Sharma says, "is to be in complete communion with them; it is to see that they have the kind of education that will help them to be sensitive, intelligent and integrated."[19]

---

16. Mugyenyi, *Aspects of Sociology*, 14.
17. Ibid., 13–14.
18. Cf. Bigner, *Parent-Child Relation*.
19. Sharma, *Problems of Education*, 152.

Conclusion

We advise teachers to clearly understand that, based on the research conducted, English language as a language of instruction has a very large contribution to the performance of students in community secondary schools. As Qorro states: "Language of instruction is a vehicle through which education is delivered. The role of language of instruction can be likened to that of pipes in carrying water from one destination to another or that of copper wires in transmitting electricity from one station to another. Just as a pipe is an important medium in carrying water, and a copper wire an important medium for transmitting electricity, the language of instruction is an indispensable medium for carrying, or transmitting education from teachers to learners and among learners."[20] It means that they should ensure that *deliberate* efforts are taken in order to make students seriously learn the language.

It would be better if English will be emphasized in Tanzania as a subject, not as LoI, and periods for English be increased both at primary and secondary levels. In addition, remedial classes can also be another option for helping students improve their English language. Teachers are also supposed to motivate students so that they may perform better in English. They may promise to reward them if they pass English examinations, and in this way students will work hard. Teachers have also the role of creating awareness to students in advance that if they shun themselves from English, it will affect all other subjects.[21] They should heed to the views of Thungu et al. that a teacher is " . . . an instructor, a motivator, an examiner or even a welfare worker."[22] For this reason, teachers have a role of motivating students and teaching them seriously in order to help them do better at their English communication skills.

Private sectors, particularly those engaged in education, should ensure that in carrying out their functions and activities in Tanzania, they play a major role in providing enough education to all Tanzanians especially to the poor communities. We advise the private sector to think of reducing school and boarding fees so that many parents may opt to take children to their schools. We are sure that most students who go to the private sector are able to perform well at Form Four because of the availability of teaching and learning materials alongside having qualified and enough teachers. The private sector is growing fast in Tanzania. Currently, there are a big number

---

20. Qorro, "Does the Language of Instruction affect Quality?" 3.
21. Cohen & Manion, *Perspectives on Classrooms*, 70–72.
22. Thungu et al., *Mastering PTE Education*, 200.

of both primary and secondary schools in Mbeya District Council and Tanzania at large. According to the DEO's information, in Mbeya District Council, for example, there are 45 secondary schools out of which 28 are community schools and the rest are private and few government secondary schools. This indicates that the private sector provides a considerable contribution towards the provision of education in Tanzania.

Strictly speaking, the use of English as a teaching and learning medium in community secondary schools in Mbeya District Council, the area of our research, has been proved to contribute greatly to students' failures in form four summative examinations. It has been found that students are not conversant in the reading, writing, understanding, and speaking areas. It was also found in the research that the areas mentioned above are in a very close connection among themselves. Most often a student who is not able to read English or understand the language is also not able to write or speak, and eventually not able to perform better in examinations. The study was conducted in Mbeya District Council; however the situation found in Mbeya District Council might be the case for all other districts in the region and in the country. As we have shown above, there are a number of partners who each has a great role to play in order to help students perform better in community secondary schools.

However, further research is required in other parts of the region and the country on this aspect of the use of English as a language of instruction, especially focusing on private and government secondary schools, colleges and universities. Forthcoming studies can also concentrate on examining how university students use English in their studies. Is English an appropriate language of instruction to college and university students in Tanzania, especially at undergraduate level? Does the use of English language as language of teaching and learning in Tanzanian colleges and universities properly prepare experts who are well-equipped to serve in a Tanzanian society whose main language of communication is Kiswahili; or it prepares graduates with a mentality of working in English speaking countries and unfit to work in the Tanzanian context? A research on these questions can help know the justification for the continuous use of the language at this level of education.

References

Aggarwal, J.C. *Principles, Methods and Techniques of Teaching*. Delhi. Vikas Publishing House, 2004.
Aggarwal, J.C. *Principles, Methods and Techniques of Teaching*. Second Revised Edition. Delhi: Vikas, 1996.
Ary, Donald, Jacobs, Lucy Cheser and Sorensen, Chris. *Introduction to Research in Education*. Belmont, CA.: Wadsworth, 2010.
Al-Bakri, Sawsan. "Problematizing English Medium Instruction in Oman." *International Journal of Bilingual and Multilingual Teachers of English* 2 (2013) 19–33.
Alphonce, Ndibalema. "The Language of Education, Literacy and Self-Identity: Implications for Tanzania." *Papers in Education and Development* 26 (2006) 130–149.
Alreck, Pamela L. and Settle, Robert B. *The Survey Research Handbook: Guidelines and Strategies for Conduction a Survey*. New York, NY.: Irwin, 1995.
Anangisye, William A.L. "Developing Quality Teacher Professionals: A Reflective inquiry on the Practices and Challenges in Tanzania," 137–154. Africa-Asia University Dialogue for Education Development Report of the International Experience Sharing Seminar (2): Actual Status and Issues of Teacher Professional Development, Hiroshima, *Centre for the Study of International Cooperation in Education (CICE)*, Hiroshima University, 2011.
Arends, Richard I. *Learning To Teach: Third Edition*. New York, NJ.: McGraw Hill, 1994.
Aveyard, Helen. *Doing Literature Review in Health and Social Care: A Practical Guide*. New York, NY.: McGraw Hill, 2007.
Azaliwa, Elifelet. "The Impact of the Medium of Instruction on Students' Academic Performance in Secondary Schools in Simanjiro District, Manyara Region: A Comparative Study."*International Journal of Education and Research* 4 (2016) 391–404.
Babaci-Wilhite, Zahlia and Geo-Jaja, Macleans A. "Localization of Instruction as a Right in Education: Tanzania and Nigeria Language-in-Education's Policies." In *Giving Space to African Voices: Rights in Local Languages and Local Curriculum*. Edited by Zahlia Babaci-Wilhite, 3–19. Rotterdam: Sense, 2013.
BAKITA. "BAKITA na Lugha ya Kufundishia." *Kioo cha Lugha: Jarida la Kiswahili la Isimu na Fasihi* 3 (2005) 1–12.

References

Batibo, Herman M. "The Growth of Kiswahili as a Language of Education and administration in Tanzania." In *Discrimination through Language in Africa? Perspectives on the Namibian Experience*, edited by M. Putz. New York, NY: Mouton de Gruyter, 1995.

Bempechat, Janine. "The Role of Parent Involvement in Children's Academic Achievement." *The School Community Journal* 2 (1992) 31–41.

Bigner, Jerry J. *Parent-Child Relations: An Introduction to Parenting*. Eighth Edition. Upper Saddle River, NJ.: Pearson Education, 2010.

Bikongoro, Peragia F. "The Relevance of the Language Policy for Instruction and Assessment of Secondary Education in Tanzania: A Comparative Analysis between the former Swahili and English Medium Students." *African Educational Research Journal* 3 (2015) 1–8.

Bogdan, Robert C. and Biklen, Sari Knopp. *Qualitative Research for Education: An Introduction to Theory and Methods*. Boston, MA.: A Viacom, 1998.

Brock-Utne, Birgit and Desai, Zubeida. "Expressing Oneself through Writing—A Comparative Study of Learners' Writing Skills in Tanzania and South Africa." In *Language of Instruction in Tanzania and South Africa–Highlights from a Project*. Edited by Birgit Brock-Utne, Zubeida Desai, Martha A.S. Qorro and Allan Pitman, 11–31. Rotterdam: Sense, 2010.

Brock-Utne, Birgit and Holmarsdottir, Halla B. "Language Policies and Practices in Tanzania and South Africa: Problems and Challenges." *HakiElimu, Working Papers Series*. Dar es Salaam, 2005.

Brock-Utne, Birgit. "Language of Instruction and Poverty Alleviation." *Papers in Education and Development* 26 (2006) 60–88.

———. "English as the Language of Instruction or Destruction–How do Teachers and Students in Tanzania Cope?" Linguistic LAUD Agency, University of Duisburg-Essen, Paper Series No. 598, 2004.

Bryman, Alan. *Quantity and Quality in Social Research*. New York, NY.: Routledge, 1988.

Bwenge, Charles. "English in Tanzania: A linguistic cultural Perspective." *International Journal of Language, Translation and Intercultural Communication* 1 (2012) 167–182.

———. "Code-Switching in Tanzanian Parliamentary Discourse: A Communicative Innovation." *Issues in Political Discourse Analysis* 2 (2008) 75–100.

———. *The Tongue Between: Swahili and English in the Tanzanian Parliamentary Discourse*. Munchen, Germany: LINCOM, 2010.

Chaube, S.P. & Chaube, A. *Foundations of Education*. Second Revised Edition. Delhi: Vikas, 2002.

———. *School Organisation: Highlighting the Basic Principles in Consonance with the Tenets of True Democracy*. Second Revised Edition. Delhi: Vikas, 2007.

Chavez, Andres. "Rights in Education and Self-Identity: Education and Language of Instruction in Namibia." *International Education Studies* 9 (2016) 189–196.

Cohen, Louis and Manion, Lawrance. *Perspectives on Classrooms and Schools*. London: Cassell Education, 1981.

Cohen, Louis, Manion, Manion, Lawrance, and Morrison, Keith. *Research in Education*. Sixth Edition. New York, NY.: Routledge, 2007.

Coombs, Bryan. *Successful Teaching: A Practical Handbook*. Ibadan: Heinenann, 1995.

Corbetta, Piergiorgio. *Social research: Theory, Methods and Techniques*. New Delhi: SAGE, 2003.

References

Creswell, J.W. *Educational Research: Planning, Conducting, and Evaluating Quantitative and Qualitative Research.* Fourth Edition. Boston, MA.: Pearson Education, 2002.

Cruickshank, Donald R, Jenkins, Deborah Bainer and Metcalf, Kim K. *The Act of Teaching.* Fifth Edition. Boston, MA.: McGraw Hill, 2009.

Evans, Jack M. and Brueckner, Martha M. *Teaching and You: Committing, Preparing and Succeeding.* Boston, MA.: Allyn and Bacon, 1992.

Dachi, H.A. "Investigating in Children's Right to Learn through the Language of Teaching and Learning: An Investment in Human Capital." *Papers in Education and Development* 26 (2006) 42–59.

Denscombe, Martyn. *The Good Research Guide for Small-Scale Social Research Projects.* Third Edition. New York, NY.: McGraw Hill, 2007.

Dzahene-Quarshie, Josephine. "Language Policy, Language Choice and Language Use in the Tanzanian Parliament." *Legon Journal of the Humanities* 22 (2011) 27–69.

Esch, Edith. "English and Empowerment: Potential, Issues, Way Forward." In *English and Empowerment in the Developing World.* Edited by Nasreen Hussain, Azra Ahmed, and Mohamad Zafar, 2–26. Cambridge: Cambridge Scholars, 2009.

Essays, UK. "Language of Instruction in Tanzania Education Essay." November, 2013. Retrieved from https://www.ukessays.com/essays/education/language-of-instruction-in-tanzania-education-essay.php?cref=1 [Accessed 07 March 2017].

Fakeye, D.O. & Ogunsuji, Y. "English Language Proficiency as a Predictor of Academic Achievement among EFL Students in Nigeria." *European Journal of Scientific Research* 37 (2009) 490–495.

Feast, V. "The Impact of IELTS Scores on Performance at University." *International Education Journal* 3 (2002) 70–85.

Fisher, Douglas and Frey, Nancy. *Checking for Understanding: Formative Assessment Techniques for Your Classroom.* Alexandria: ASCB Member Book, 2007.

Freire, Paulo. *Pedagogy of the Oppressed.* Revised Twentieth-Anniversary Edition. New York, NY.: Continuum, 1993.

Gathumbi, Agnes W. and Masembe, Ssebbunga C. *Principles and Techniques in Language Teaching: A Text for Teacher Educators, Teachers and Pre-service Teachers.* Nairobi: Jomo Kenyatta Foundation, 2005.

———. *Principles and Techniques in Language Teaching.* Nairobi: Icons, 2008.

Gawasike, Arnold. "Lugha ya Kiswahili katika Kutandawaza Maarifa Tanzania: Mtazamo wa Ubeberu wa Kiisimu." *Journal of Teofilo Kisanji University* 5 (2015) 69–81.

Gawi, Elsadig Mohamed Khalifa. "The Effects of Age Factor on Learning English: A Case Study of Learning English in Saudi Schools, Saudi Arabia." *English Language Teaching* 5 (2012) 128–139.

Gran, Line Kjorstad. "Language of Instruction in Tanzanian Higher Education: A Particular Focus on the University of Dar es Salaam." M. Phil. Thesis, University of Oslo, Oslo Norway, 2007.

Hardman, Frank. "A Review of Teacher Education in Tanzania and the Potential for closer links between PRESET and INSET." A Report produced in Support to the Ministry of Education and Vocational Training (MoEVT) for the Development of an INSET Strategy and Development Plan linked to the Teacher Development and Management Strategy (TDMS) 2008–2013. Dar es Salaam Tanzania, 2009.

Hart, Chris. *Doing literature Review: Releasing the Social Science Research Imagination.* London: SAGE, 1998.

References

Hurskainen, Arvi. "Kiswahili na Hali Halisi katika Tekinolojia ya Lugha." *Kiswahili: Journal of the Institute of Kiswahili Research* 68 (2005) 115–127.

Jackson, Cynthia L. *African American Education: A Reference Handbook.* ABC-CLIO, 2001.

John, Julitha Cecilia. "What is the Difference in the Quality of Education provided by Government and Private Primary Schools in Tanzania?" Master Thesis in Comparative and International Education, University of Oslo, Oslo Norway, 2009.

Jonker, Jan and Pennink, Bartjan. *The Essence of Research Methodology: A Concise Guide for Master and PhD Students in Management Science.* Berlin: Springer, 2010.

Kadeghe, Michael. "Code-Switching in Tanzanian Classrooms: Asset or Liability?" *Papers in Education and Development* 26 (2006) 116–129.

———. "In Defence of Continued Use of English as the Language of Instruction in Secondary and Tertiary Education in Tanzania." In *Language of Instruction in Tanzania and South Africa–Highlights from a Project.* Edited by Birgit Brock-Utne, Zubeida Desai, Martha A.S. Qorro and Allan Pitman, pp. 61–76. Rotterdam: Sense, 2010.

Kalmanlehto, Iida. "Mixed domains and multilingual practices-an ethnographic study of Tanzanian university students' language use." M.Thesis, Social Anthropology. University of Tampere, 2012.

Kapoli, Ireneus Joseph. "The Effects of Interaction on the Writing of English Composition: An Exploratory Study in Secondary Schools in Tanzania." PhD Thesis, University of London, London England, 1992.

Kellough, Richard D. *Surviving Your First Year of Teaching: Guidelines for Success.* New Jersey, NJ.: Prentice Hall, 1999.

Khamisi, Abdu Mtajuka. "Kiswahili ikiwa ni Lugha ya Kimataifa." In *Lugha ya Kiswahili: Makala za Semina ya Kimataifa ya Waandihi wa Kiswahili*, 1–18. Dar es Salaam: Uchunguzi wa Kiswahili, 2010.

Kimizi, Moshi M. "Why has the Language of Instruction Policy in Tanzania been so Ambivalent over the Last Forty Years? A Study Eliciting Views from Government Policy-Makers, International Donors to Tanzania, University Academics and Researchers, and the General Public." Master Thesis in Comparative and International Education, University of Oslo, Oslo Norway, 2007.

Kinyaduka, Bryson D. and Kiwara, Joyce F. "Language of Instruction and its Impact on Quality of Education in Secondary Schools: Experiences from Morogoro Region, Tanzania" *Journal of Education and Practice* 4 (2013) 90–95.

Kitta, Septimi and Fussy, Daniel. "Bottlenecks in Preparation of Quality Teachers in Tanzania." *Time Journals of Arts and Educational Research* 1 (2013) 29–38.

Komba, Setco Claudius, Kafanabo, Eugenia Joseph, Njabili, Agnes Fellicia, & Kira, Ernest S. "Comparison between Students' academic Performance and Their Abilities in written English Language Skills: A Tanzanian Perspective." *International Journal of Development Sustainability* 1 (2012) 305–325.

Komba, Setco Claudius and John, Daimana. "Investigation of Pupils' English Language Abilities in Tanzania: The Case of English Medium Primary Schools." *World Journal of English Language* 5 (2015) 56—64.

Komba, Setco Claudius and Bosco, Stephen. "Do Students' Backgrounds in the Language of Instruction Influence Secondary School Academic Performance?" *Journal of Education and Practice* 6 (2015) 148–156.

References

Komba, Willy L. and Nkumbi, Emmanuel. "Teacher Professional Development in Tanzania: Perceptions and Practices." *Journal of International Cooperation in Education* 1 (2008) 67–83.

Kombo, Donald Kisilu and Tromp, Delno L.A. *Proposal and Thesis Writing: An Introduction.* Nairobi: Paulines Publication Africa., 2006

Kothari, C.K. *Research Methodology: Methods and Techniques.* New Delhi: New Age International, 2004.

Koul, Lokesh. *Methodology of Educational Research.* New Delhi: Vikas, 1984.

Kronowitz, Ellen L. *Beyond Student Teaching.* Toronto: Longman, 1991.

Langan, John. *Reading and Study Skills.* 7th Edition. Boston, MA.: McGraw Hill, 2002.

Legere, Karsten. "Uwezeshwaji wa Kiswahili Siku Hizi: Mafanikio na Matatizo." *Kiswahili: Journal of the Institute of Kiswahili Research* 68 (2005) 150–162.

———. "*Marehemu* Julius Kambarage Nyerere and Kiswahili." *Kioo cha Lugha: Jarida la Kiswahili la Isimu na Fasihi* 5 (2007) 39—42.

Lyimo, Godrick Ephraim. "Analysis of Teachers' Low Payments in Tanzania: A Case Study of Public Secondary Schools in Moshi Rural District." *International Journal of Education and Research* 2 (2014) 1–14.

Lund, Thorleif. "The Qualitative-Quantitative Distinction: Some Comments." *Scandinavian Journal of Educational Research* 49 (2005) 115–132.

Lupogo, Issaya. "The Intensity of Language of Instruction Problem in Tanzanian Universities: Is it a Numeracy and Literacy Background Case?" *Pyrex Journal of Educational Research and Reviews* 2 (2016) 48–54.

Makewa, Lazarus Ndiku, Role, Elizabeth and Tuguta, Ellen. "Students' Perceived Level of English Proficiency in Secondary Schools in Dodoma, Tanzania." *International Journal of Instruction* 6 (2013) 35–52.

Makgato, Moses. "The Use of English and Code Switching in the Teaching and Learning of Technology in some Schools in Eastern Cape Province, South Africa." *Mediterranean Journal of Social Sciences* 5 (2014) 933–930.

Manh, Le Duc. "English as a Medium of Instruction in Asian Universities: The Case of Vietnam." *Language Education in Asia* 6 (2012) 263–267.

Machi, Laurence A. & McEvoy, Brenda T. *The Literature Review: Six Steps to Success.* Thousand Oaks, CA.: SAGE, 2009.

Makunja, Grace. "Challenges Facing Teachers in Implementing Competence-Based Curriculum in Tanzania: The Case of Community Secondary Schools in Morogoro Municipality." *International Journal of Education and Social Sciences* 3 (2016) 30–37.

Maleki, A. and Zangani, E. "A Survey on the Relationship between English Language Proficiency and the academic Achievement of Iranian EFL Students." *Asian EFL Journal* 9 (2007) 86–96.

Marwa, Nyankomo W. Tanzania's Language of Instruction Policy Dilemma: Is there a Solution?" *Mediterranean Journal of Social Sciences* 5 (2014) 1262–1268.

Marzano, Robert J., Pickering, Debra J. and Pollock, Jane E. *Classroom Instruction that Works.* Alexandria: ASCD Publication, 2001.

Masele, B.F.Y.P. "Kiswahili au Kiingereza? Siasa na Lugha Muafaka ya Kufundishia Tanzania." *Kioo cha Lugha: Jarida la Kiswahili la Isimu na Fasihi* 3 (2005) 31–50.

Masudi, Abuhashimu. "The need for an Appropriate Medium for Instruction in Secondary Education and Institutions of Higher Learning in Tanzania." *Papers in Education and Development* 26 (2006) 32–41.

References

Mchumbo, Sam. "Language, Learning, and Education for All in Africa." In *Giving Space to African Voices: Rights in Local Languages and Local Curriculum*. Edited by Zahlia Babaci-Wilhite, 21-46. Rotterdam: Sense, 2013.

Mcnegney, Robert F. and Herbert, Joanne M. *Foundations of Education: The Challenge of Professional Practice*. Boston, MA.: Allyn and Bacon, 1995.

Mgqwashu, Emmanuel. "Language and the Postcolonial Condition." *Alternation* 13 (2006) 298-325.

Mkumbo, Kitila A.K. "Teachers' Commitment to, and Experiences of, the Teaching Profession in Tanzania: Findings of Focus Group Research." *International Education Studies* 5 (2012) 222-227.

Mlay, Neema. "The Influence of the Language of Instruction on Students' Academic Performance in Secondary Schools: A Comparative Study of Urban and Rural Schools in Arusha Tanzania." Master of Philosophy Thesis in Comparative and International Education. University of Oslo, Oslo Norway, 2010.

Mligo, Elia Shabani. *Introduction to Research Methods and Report Writings: A Practical Guide for Students and Researchers in Social Sciences and the Humanities*. Eugene, OR.: Wipf and Stock/Resource, 2016.

———. *Symbolic Interactionism in the Gospel according to John: A Contextual Study of the Symbolism of Water*. Eugene, OR.: Wipf and Stock, 2014.

———. *Doing Effective Fieldwork: A Textbook for Students of Qualitative Field Research in Higher-Learning Institutions*. Eugene, OR.: Wipf and Stock/Resource, 2013.

Mochiwa, Z.S.M. "Kiswahili kwa Kufundishia: Sera na Mikakati." *Kioo cha Lugha: Jarida la Kiswahili la Isimu na Fasihi* 3 (2005) 51-65.

Modupeola, Olagunju Robert. "Code-Switching as a teaching strategy: Implication for English Language teaching and learning in a multilingual society." *IOSR Journal of Humanities and Social Science* 14 (2013) 92-94.

Mouton, Johann. *How to Succeed in Your Master's and Doctoral Studies: A South African Resource and Guide Book*. Pretoria: Van Schaik, 2001.

Msanjila, Yohana P. "Dhima ya Lugha ya Kiswahili katika Karne ya Ishirini na Moja." *Kiswahili: Journal of the Institute of Kiswahili Research* 65 (2002) 16-23.

———. "Kiswahili kutumika katika Umoja wa Afrika: Changamoto na Mikakati ya Utekelezaji." *Kiswahili: Journal of the Institute of Kiswahili Research* 68 (2005) 94-102.

———. "Hali ya Kiswahili katika Shule za Sekondari Tanzania: Udhalilishaji wa Lugha ya Taifa?" *Swahili Forum* 12 (2005) 205-218.

Msuya, Ombeni William. "Exploring Levels of Job Satisfaction among Teachers in Public Secondary Schools in Tanzania." *International Journal of Educational Administration and Policy Studies* 8 (2016) 9-16.

Mtallo, Godson Robert. "Teaching and Learning English in Tanzania: Blessing or Curse? A Practical Review of Phan le Ha's Teaching English as an International Language." *Journal of Education and Practice* 6 (2015) 118-123.

Mtesigwa, P. "Utandawazi na Dhima ya Kiswahili kama Lugha ya Afrika ya Mashariki." *Kioo cha Lugha: Jarida la Kiswahili la Isimu na Fasihi* 3 (2005) 66-75.

Muganda, C.K., Kanuwa, M.J. & Mwereke, T.T. "Introduction to Education Foundations." Dar es Salaam, 2008 (Unpublished Paper).

Mugyenyi, Apolo A. *Aspects of Sociology, Philosophy Management and Administration*. Moshi: Moshi Printing Press, 2013.

References

Mulokozi, M.M. "Baadhi ya Vipingamizi vya Kiutawala vya Kutumia Kiswahili Kufundisha Sekondari na Vyuo." *Kioo cha Lugha: Jarida la Kiswahili la Isimu na Fasihi* 3 (2005)13–21.

———. "Kiswahili as a National and International Language." *Kiswahili: Journal of the Institute of Kiswahili Research* 66 (2003) 66–80.

Mwinsheikhe, Halima. "Using Kiswahili as Medium of Instruction in Science teaching in Tanzanian Secondary Schools," pp. 129–148. In *Language of Instruction in Tanzania and South Africa (LOITASA)*, edited by Brock-Utne, Birgit, Desai, Zubeida and Qorro, Martha, 129–148. Dar-es-salaam: E & D, 2003.

Mwansoko, H.J.M. Mchango wa Mwalimu J.K.Nyerere katika Tafsiri na Maendeleo ya Lugha." *Kioo cha Lugha: Jarida la Kiswahili la Isimu na Fasihi* 3 (2005) 76–81.

Mwipopo, Marko J. "Secondary School Graduates' Personal Experiences in the Context of English-Only Language of Instruction Within and Outside the School Setting in Tanzania." PhD Thesis, University of Oregon, United States of America, 2016.

Myra, Pollack, and Sadker, David Miller. *Teachers, Schools and Society*. Seventh Edition. New York, NY.: McGraw-Hill, 2005.

Narardi, Peter M. *Doing Survey Research: A Guide to Quantitative Methods*. Boston, MA.: Pearson Education, 2003.

Ndalichako, Joyce Lazaro and Komba, Aneth Anselmo. "Students' Subject Choice in Secondary Schools in Tanzania: A Matter of Students' Ability and Interests or Forced Circumstances?" *Open Journal of Social Sciences* 2 (2014) 49–56. Online at: http://dx.doi.org/10.4236/jss.2014.28008.

Ndalichako, Joyce Lazaro. "Analysis of Pupils' Difficulties in Solving Questions Related to Fractions: The Case of Primary School Leaving Examination in Tanzania." *Creative Education* 4 (2013) 69–73.

Neke, Stephen Mueta. "English in Tanzania: An Anatomy of the Hegemony." PhD Thesis, Universiteit Gent, Belgium, 2003.

———. "The Medium of Instruction in Tanzania: Reflections on Language, Education and Society." *Changing English: Studies in Culture and Education* 12 (2005): 73–83.

Nel, Norma and Muller, Helene. "The Impact of Teachers' limited English Proficiency on English Second Language Learners in South African Schools." *South African Journal of Education* 30 (2010) 635–650.

Neuman, W.L. *Basics of Social Research: Qualitative and Quantitative Approaches*. Second Edition. Boston, MA.: Pearson Education, 2007.

Ngaroga, J.M. *Professional Studies for Secondary Teacher Education: Revision*. Nairobi: East African Educational Publishers, 1996.

Nyamubi, Gilman Jackson. "Students' Attitudes and English Language Performance in Secondary Schools in Tanzania." *International Journal of Learning, Teaching and Educational Research* 15 (2016) 117–133.

Ngimbudzi, Fred Wilson. "Job Satisfaction among Secondary School Teachers in Tanzania: The Case of Njombe District." Master Thesis in Education. University of Jyvaskyla, Finland, 2009.

Njabili, Agnes F. *Public Examinations: A Tool for Curriculum, Evaluation*. Third Edition. Dar es salaam: Mture Educational Publishers, 1999.

Nomlomo, Vuyokazi and Vuzo, Mwajuma. "Language Transition and Access to Education: Experiences from Tanzania and South Africa." *International Journal of Educational Studies* 1 (2014) 73–82.

References

Nyerere, Julius Kambarage. *Education for Self-Relience.* Dar es Salaam: Government Printer, 1967.

Oluoch, G.P. *Essentials of Curriculum Development.* Revised Edition. Nairobi: Birds Printers Office & Stationary & Equipment, 1982.

Onsumu, Eldah Nyamoita, et al. (2004). *Community Schools in Kenya: Case Study on Community Participation in Funding and Managing Schools.* Paris: UNESCO.

Ouane, Adama and Glanz, Christine, *Why and How Africa should Invest in African Languages and Multilingual Education: An Evidence-and Practice-based Policy Advocacy Brief.* UNESCO Institute for Life Long Learning, 2010.

Persson, Mikaela. "'It's like going fishing without a fishing-net': A Study on How Students in Tanzania perceive the Transition of Language of Instruction from Kiswahili to English." Master Thesis, Hogskolan Kristianstad, 2013.

Petzell, Malin. "The Linguistic Situation in Tanzania." *Mordena Sprak* 1 (2012) 136–144.

Phillipson, Robert. *Linguistic Imperialism.* New York, NY.: Oxford University Press, 1992.

PlonskiL, Patrick, Teferra, Asratie and Brady, Rachel. "Why Are More African Countries Adopting English as an Official Language?" A Paper Presented at African Studies Association Annual Conference, November 23, 2013. Baltimore, Maryland, 2013.

Pitman, Allan, Majhanovich, Suzanne and Brock-Utne, Birgit. "English as a Language of Instruction in Africa." In *Language of Instruction in Tanzania and South Africa-Highlights from a Project,* edited by Birgit Brock-Utne, Zubeida Desai, Martha A.S. Qorro and Allan Pitman, 1–10. Rotterdam: Sense Publishers, 2010.

Probyn, M.J. "Teachers' Voices: Teachers Reflections on Learning and Teaching through the Medium of English as a Second Language." *International Journal of Bilingual Education and Bilingualism* 4 (2001) 249–266.

Qorro, Martha. "A Qualitative Study on Teaching and Writing in Tanzania Secondary Schools in Relation to Writing Requirements of Tertiary Education." PhD Thesis, University of Dar es Salaam, Tanzania, 1999.

———. "Language of Instruction not Determinant in Quality Education." *Guardian,* Wednesday, 29 May, 2002.

———. "Language of Instruction in Tanzania: Why Research Findings are not Heeded?" *International Review of Education* 59 (2013) 29–45.

———. "Matatizo ya Kutumia Kiingereza Kufundishia katika Shule za Sekondari na Vyuo vya Juu." *Kioo cha Lugha: Jarida la Kiswahili la Isimu na Fasihi* 3 (2005) 22–30.

———. "Language of Instruction and Its effects on the Quality of Education." *Papers in Education and Development* 27 (2007) 56–78.

———. "Does Language of Instruction affect Quality of Education?" *HakiElimu. Working Papers Series.* Dar es Salaam Tanzania, 2006.

Quist, Dawn. *Primary Teaching Methods.* London: Macmillan Education Limited, 2000.

Rubagumya, Casmir M. "English-Medium Instruction in Tanzanian Secondary Schools: A Conflict of Aspirations and Achievements." *Language, Curriculum and Culture* 2 (2009): 107–115.

———. "Language Values of Tanzanian Secondary School Pupils: A Case Study in Dar es Salaam Region." Unpublished Ph.D. Thesis, Lancaster University, 1993.

Rugemalira, Josephat M. "Theoretical and Practical Challenges in a Tanzanian English Medium Primary School." *Africa and Asia* 5 (2005). 66–84.

Ryanga, Sheila. "The African Union in the Wake of Globalization: The forgotten Language Dimension." *Kiswahili: Journal of the Institute of Kiswahili Research* 65 (2002) 1–15.

References

Sa, Eleuthera. "Language Policy for Education and Development in Tanzania." 1–28. Online at www.swarthmore.edu/sites/default/files/assets/documents/linguistics/2007_sa_eleuthera.pdf [Accessed 13 March, 2017].

Savage, Tom V., Savage, Marsha K. and Amstrong, David G. *Teaching in the Secondary School.* New Jersey. Pearson Merrill Prentice Hall, 2006.

Senkoro, F.E.M.K. "Language of Instruction: The Forgotten Factor in Education Quality and Standard in Africa?" Paper Presented at CODESRIA General Assembly, Maputo, Mozambique, 2005.

Sharma, Promila. *Problems of Education.* New Delhi: A.P.H. Publishing Cooperation, 2005.

Sifuna, Daniel N. and Otiende, James E. *An Introductory History of Education*: Revised Edition. Nairobi: Nairobi University Press, 1992.

Sodhi, T.S. *Textbook of Comparative Education.* Sixth Edition. New Delhi: Vikas, 1998.

Snow, Don. *From Language Learner to Language Teacher: An Introduction to Teaching English as a Foreign Language.* Michigan: Teachers of English to Speakers of Other Languages, 2007.

Sumra, Suleman and Katabaro, Jovita K. *Declining Quality of Education: Suggestions for Arresting and Reversing the Trend.* Dar es Salaam: Economic and Social Research Foundation, 2014.

Sumra, Suleman and Rajani, Rakesh. "Secondary Education in Tanzania: Key Policy Challenges." *HakiElimu Tanzania,* Dar es Salaam, 2006.

Swilla, Imani N. "Languages of Instruction in Tanzania: Contradictions between Ideology, Policy and Implementation." *African Study Monographs* 30 (2009) 1– 4.

Telli, Geofrey. "The Language of Instruction Issue in Tanzania: Pertinent Determining Factors and Perception of Education Stakeholders." *Journal of Languages and Culture* 5 (2014) 9–16.

Toft, Doug and Mancina, Dean. *Becoming a Master Student.* Thirteenth Edition. Boston, MA: Wadsworth Cengage Learning, 2011.

Thomas, Ellen Lamar and Robinson, H.Alan (1972). *Improving Reading in Every Class.* Abridged Edition. Boston, MA.: Allyn and Bacon.

Thungu, Jane, Wandera, Kezziah, Gachie, Lizzie and Alumande, Gladys. *Mastering PTE Education.* New York, NY.: Oxford University Press, 2011.

Tibategeza, Eustard Rutalemwa. "Implementation of Bilingual Education in Tanzania: The Realities in Schools." *Nordic Journal of African Studies* 19 (2010) 227–249.

Tileston, Dinna Walker. *What Every Teacher Should Know about Students Motivation.* California. Corwin Press, A SAGE Publication Company, 2004.

Towse, P., Kent, D., Osaki, F. & Kirua, F. "Non-graduate Teacher Recruitment and Retention: Some Factors affecting Teacher Effectiveness in Tanzania." *Teacher and Teacher Education* 18 (2002) 637–652.

URT. *Education and Training Policy.* Ministry of Education and Culture. Dar es Salaam, 1995.

———. *Sera ya Utamaduni,* Ministry of Education and Culture, Dar es Salaam, 1997.

———. *Cultural Policy Statements.* Ministry of Education and Culture, Dar es Salaam, 1997.

———. *The Tanzania Development Vision 2025.* Dar es Salaam, Planning Commission, 2000.

———. *Sera ya Elimu.* Ministry of Education and Culture. Dar es Salaam, 2014.

References

———. *Education Sector Development Programme: Secondary Education Development Programme II July 2010–June 2015*. Ministry of Education and Culture. Dar es Salaam, 2010.

Uys, Mandie, Walt, Johann van der, Berg, Ria van den and Botha, Sue. "English as a Medium of Instruction: A Situation Analysis." *South African Journal of Education*. Volume 27 (2015) 69–82.

Vuzo, Mwajuma. "Stakeholders' Opinions on the Use of Code Switching/Code Mixing as Coping Strategies and Its Implications for Teaching and Learning in Tanzanian Secondary Schools." *Huria: Journal of the Open University of Tanzania*.11 (2012) 127–144.

Vyhmeister, Nancy Jean. *Quality Research Papers: For Students of Religion and Theology*. Grand Rapids, Michigan: Zondervan, 2008.

Wamalwa, Eric W., Adika, Stanley K., and Kevogo, Alex U. "Multilingualism and Language Attitudes: Students Perceptions towards Kiswahili in Mtwara Region of Tanzania." *Research on Humanities and Social Sciences* 3 (2013) 53–65.

Wierzbicka, Anna, *English: Meaning and Culture*. New York, NY.: Oxford University Press, 2006.

Wikipedia, "Education in Tanzania." Online at https://en.wikipedia.org/wiki/Education_in_Tanzania [Accessed 07 March 2017].

Wilson, Job and Komba, Sotco Claudius. "The Link between English Language Proficiency and Academic Performance: A Pedagogical Perspective in Tanzanian Secondary Schools." *World Journal of English Language* 2 (2012) 1–10.

Wong, Ruth M. H. "The Effectiveness of Using English as the Sole Medium of Instruction in English Classes: Student Responses and Improved English Proficiency." *Porta Linguarum* 13 (2010) 199–130.

Yao, Ju. "A Study of the Teaching and Learning of English Grammar in the Chinese Junior Secondary School." M. Phil. Dissertation. University of Oslo, Oslo Norway, 2010.

Yoradi, Sikombe Yizukanji. "Lugha ya Kiswahili katika Kufundishia na Kujifunzia Elimu Shule za Sekondari." MA (Kiswahili) Thesis. The Open University of Tanzania, Dar es Salaam, 2013.

Name Index

Aggarwal, J. C., 116, 116n65
Al-Bakri, Sawsan, 37, 37n16
Alphonce, Ndibalema, 33n3
Alreck, Pamela L., 62, 62n24
Alumande, Gladys, 101n41, 102, 102n43, 107, 107n51
Amstrong, David G., 120n72
Arends, Richard I., 115, 115n64
Ary, Donald, 55, 55n4

Babaci-Wilhite, Zahlia, 11n20, 15, 15n34, 86n12
Batibo, Herman M., xv, xvn7
Bempechat, Janine, 131, 131n15
Bigner, Jerry J., 132n18
Biklen, Sari Knopp, 56, 60, 60n14
Bikongoro, Peragia F., 24n56
Blumer, Herbert, 58
Bogdan, Robert C., 56, 60, 60n14
Bosco, Stephen, 38, 39n20
Brady, Rachel, 33, 33n4
Brock-Utne, Birgit, 12n24, 85, 85n11, 89, 89n18, 95n29, 106, 106n49
Brueckner, Martha M., 90, 90n21, 92, 92n23
Bryman, Alan, 57n8
Bwenge, Charles, 21n45, 27n66

Chaube, A., 113, 113n59, 119, 119n71
Chaube, S. P., 113, 113n59, 119, 119n71

Chavez, Andres, 44, 44n25
Cohen, Louis, 54, 57n9 67n2, 133n21
Comte, Auguste, 57
Coombs, Bryan, 114, 114n60
Corbetta, Piergiorgio, 57, 57n9, 58
Creswell, J. W., 58, 58n13

Desai, Zubeida, 95n29, 106, 106n49
Dilthey, Wilhelm, 58
Dzahene-Quarshie, Josephine, 12n28

Esch, Edith, 68, 68n3
Evans, Jack M., 90, 90n21, 92, 92n23

Fakeye, D. O., 123n2
Fisher, Douglas, 104, 104n45
Freire, Paulo, 65, 65n26
Frey, Nancy, 104, 104n45
Fussy, Daniel, 126, 126n4, 127, 127n6, 128, 128n8, 129, 130, 130n12

Gachie, Lizzie, 101n41, 102, 102n43, 107, 107n51
Gathumbi, Agnes W., 105, 105n46, 116, 116n65
Gawasike, Arnold, 51, 51n37
Gawi, Elsadig Mohamed Khalifa, 40, 87, 87n14
Geo-Jaja, Macleans A., 11n20, 15, 86n12
Glanz, Christine, 11n19

Name Index

Gran, Line Kjolstad, 11n21, 12n27, 16n39, 47

Hardman, Frank, 127n6
Holmasdottir, 12n24
Hurskainen, Arvi, 95n32, 96

Jackson, Cynthia L., 111, 111n57, 114
Jacobs, Lucy Cheser, 55, 55n4
John, Julitha Cecilia, 40n24, 45, 46

Kadeghe, Michael, 48
Kalmanlehto, Iida, 12n24
Kapoli, Ireneus Joseph, 15n36
Katabaro, Jovita K., 126n5, 130n13
Kawawa, Rashid, 12, 12n26
Kellough, Richard D., 106, 106n50, 119, 119n68
Khamisi, Abdu Mtajuka, 12n24
Kimizi, Moshi M., 6, 6n3, 12n24, 14n32, 15n33, 21n46, 34, 34n6, 120, 120n73
Kitta, Septimi, 126, 126n4, 127, 127n6, 128, 128n8, 129, 130, 130n12
Komba, Setco Claudius, 38, 39n20, 40n24, 45, 46, 49, 50n36, 85, 85n10, 88n17, 95, 95n31, 103, 104
Kombo, Donald Kisilu, 56, 60, 60n16
Kothari, C. K., 62, 62n23
Koul, Lokesh, 55, 55n2
Kronowitz, Ellen L., 119, 119n69

Legere, Karsten, 13n29
Lund, Thorleif, 57, 57n10
Lupogo, Issaya, 98, 98n38
Lyimo, Godrick Ephraim, 120n11

Machi, Laurence A., 31n1
Majhanovich, Suzanne, 85, 85n11, 89
Makewa, Lazarus Ndiku, 50
Makgato, Moses, 87, 87n14
Makunja, Grace, 88, 88n16, 100, 101n40, 106, 106n48
Makweta, Jackson, 125

Mancina, Dean, 114, 115, 115n63
Manh, Le Duc, 36, 36n15, 37
Manion, Lawrance, 67, 133n21
Marwa, Nyankomo W., 14n31, 24n57, 26n61
Marzano, Robert J., 109, 109n55
Masembe, Ssebbunga C., 105, 105n46, 116, 116n65
McEvoy, Brenda T., 31n1
Mchumbo, Sam, 1n1
Mead, George Herbert, 58
Mgqwashu, Emmanuel, 13n30, 14n30
Mlay, Neema, 9n11, 33n5, 50n36, 90, 112n58
Mligo, Elia Shabani, 2–5, 31n1, 54n1, 55n3, 56, 60, 60n17, 61, 61n21, 67
Mochiwa, Z. S. M., 9n14
Modupeola, Olagunju Robert, 82n9
Msanjila, Yohana P., 49, 49n34
Msuya, Ombeni William, 19, 19n42
Mtallo, Godson Robert, 46, 48
Muganda, C. K., Kanuwa, 21n47, 22n52, 22n53
Mugyenyi, Apolo A., 6n4, 9, 9n10, 9n12, 10n15, 131, 131n14, 132, 132n16
Muller, Helene, 43
Mulokozi, 10n19, 25, 25n59, 27, 27n67, 27n68, 28n69, 95, 95n30
Mwipopo, Marko J., 86, 88n17, 93, 93n24, 98n37, 110, 110n56
Myra, Pollack, 91, 91n22

Ndalichako, Joyce Lazaro, 9n11, 19n41, 49, 50n36, 85, 85n10, 95, 95n31, 103, 104
Neke, Stephen Mugeta, 27, 27n65
Nel, Norma, 43
Newton, Isaac, 31
Ngaroga, J. M., 8n8
Ngimbudzi, Fred Wilson, 21n48
Nyerere, Julius K., 9, 12, 12n26
Ogunsuji, Y., 123n2
Otiende, James E., 7, 7n6
Ouane, Adama, 11n19

Name Index

Person, Mikaela, 25, 25n58
Phan Le Ha, 46
Phillipson, Robert, xiv, xvn5, 35, 35n10, 36, 36n13
Pitman, Allan, 85, 85n11, 89, 89n18
Plonski, Patrick, 33, 33n4
Probyn, M. J., 82n9

Qorro, Martha, 7, 7n7, 10n18, 23n55, 28n70, 29n71, 34, 34n6, 39, 39n21, 40n23, 105n47, 121n74, 123n2, 133, 133n20

Rajani, Rakesh, 129n10
Role, Elizabeth, 50
Rugemalira, Josephat M., 89
Ryanga, Sheila, 10n19

Sa, Eleuthera, 11n23, 12n24, 45n26
Sandker, 91, 91n22
Sarungi, Philemon M., 129
Savage, Marsha K., 120, 120n72
Savage, Tom V, 120, 120n72
Senkoro, F. E. M. K., 26, 26n64
Settle, Robert B., 62, 62n24
Sharma, Promila, 96n33, 98, 99n39, 132, 132n19
Sifuna, Daniel N., 7, 7n6
Snow, Don, 98n36, 99, 109n54
Sorensen, Chris, 55, 55n4

Sumra, Suleman, 126n5, 129n10, 130n13
Swilla, Imani N., 8n9, 12n24, 20, 20n44

Teferra, Asratie, 33, 33n4
Telli, Godfrey, 10n17, 15, 15n35, 22n49, 36, 36n13, 38n17
Thungu, Jane, 101n41, 102, 102n43, 107, 107n51, 133n22
Tileston, Dinna Walker, 119n67
Toft, Doug, 114, 115n63
Towse, P., 130n12
Tromp, Delno, 56, 60, 60n16
Tuguta, Ellen, 50

Uys, Mandie, 43

Vuzo, Mwajuma Siama, 47, 93, 94, 94n26, 97, 102, 108, 108n53

Wandera, Kezziah, 101n41, 102, 102n43, 107, 107n51
Weber, Max, 58
Wierzbicka, Anna, 2n2
Wilson, Job, 88n17
Wong, Ruth M. H., 38, 38n18, 38n19

Yao, Ju, 41, 42
Yoradi, Sikombe Yizukanji, 46

Subject Index

Page numbers followed by n indicate notes.

Adult Education (1970), 10
advanced secondary education under NECTA, 18
African Americans, culture affecting learning among, 111
African indigenous education, 6–8
Arabic, academic studies in, 37
Arabs in Tanzania, 8, 11
Arusha Declaration, 9–10

BAKITA (National Kishwahili Council), 16
banking education, 65n26, 88–89
Basic Educational Statistics in Tanzania (BEST), 127
behavioral gap due to language, 27–28

Cantonese, academic studies in, 38
certificate level education, 18
China, learning English language in, 41–42
Christianity, changing to, 8–9
code mixing, 47–48, 82, 116–17
code switching, 47–48, 82, 94, 97, 116–17
colonial education, 8–9
communication between teachers and parents, 119

community members, sensitization of, 131
community secondary schools in Kenya, 23
community secondary schools in Tanzania, 21–24. *See also* secondary education systems
  Government efforts to improve, 23–24
  history, 21–22
  implementation, 21–22
  operation, 22–23
  problems, 24–26
competence-based curriculum, 88, 100, 106
convenience sampling, 63
cultural gap due to language, 27–28
cultural identity, rejecting, 9, 118
Cultural Policy of 1997, 15, 16
culture affecting learning among African Americans, 111
curriculum implementer, 48

data
  analysis and presentation, 63–64
  collection, instruments for, 63
debate competitions and language development, 116

149

Subject Index

diploma education under NACTE, 18

East African Community (EAC), 125
economic conditions in rural areas, 5
education
    as defined by Qorro, 7
    as defined by Sifuna & Otiende, 7
    development of, 95n32
    in history of Tanzania, 6–10
    and Kishwahili, 10–21
    in rural areas, 5
Education and Training Act No.10, 21
Education and Training Policy (1995), 10
Education for Self-Reliance policy (ESR), 9, 27
elitism and English, 20–21, 33. *See also* English as a medium for teaching and learning
English, study and use of, 84–99
    academic performance, 84–86
    ages of respondents, 86–87
    availability of books, 87–89
    language proficiency and students' failure in examinations, 92–95
    teachers' availability, 89–91
    teachers' fluency in English language, 96–99
    teachers' teaching experiences, 91–92
English as a language of teaching and learning, investigating the impact of using, 55–65
    area of study and sources of data, 59–61
    data analysis and presentation, 63–64
    hypothesis and design, 55–59
    instruments for data collection, 63
    population and sample, 62–63
English as a medium for teaching and learning, 18, 32–35, 115–21
    English as international language, 32–33
    English Language Teaching Support Project (ELTSP), 34–35
    reasons for learning English, 33–34

English language and students' academic performance, 99–107
    students' ability to listen and understand English language, 103–5
    students' ability to read English language, 99–101
    students' ability to speak English language, 101–3
    students' ability to write English, 105–7
English language anxiety among Tanzanian students, 50
English language at a global level, 35–42
    age factor and English proficiency, 40
    in China, 41–42
    in Hong Kong, 38
    lack of English proficiency among teachers, 39–42
    in Oman, 37
    problems in English proficiency, 36–37
    in Saudi Arabia, 40
    teachers' proficiency contributing to students', 39
    in Vietnam, 36, 38
English language in Africa, 43–45
English language in Tanzania, 45–51
    code switching and code mixing by teachers, 47–48
    effectiveness of English language as a medium of instruction, 45–46
    English language anxiety, 50
    fees in English medium schools, 46
    Kiswahili, excessive use of, 50–51
    negative attitude towards English, 49–50
    speaking skills, 50
    trans-lingualism, 48
English Language Teaching Support Project (ELTSP), 34–35
English learning materials, 116
English proficiency
    among teachers, lack of, 39–42
    problems in, 36–37
    teachers' proficiency contributing to students', 39

Subject Index

English teachers
    competency of, 120
    lack of competent, 118. *See also* teachers
    shortage of, 110–11
essay writing competitions, 118
ethnic groups, informal education for, 6
European colonizers, 8–9
evil mentality *(kasumba)*, 27–28
exercises for English learning, 41
experience, 92

family conflicts and poverty, student's poor performance and, 114
Focus Group Discussions (FGDs), 61
foreign language, 65n26, 95n32
formal education
    challenges in, 9
    initiation of, 8
form four examinations, students' poor performance in, 113–15

German colonial rule (1886–1919), 11
government secondary schools, 6, 18

"Harambee Schools", 23
Hong Kong, English language in, 38
hypothesis, defined, 55

informal education, 6–8
Institute for Kiswahili Research, 16
interactionism, 57–58
interviews, 61
"Investigation of Pupils' English Language Abilities in Tanzania," 45
isXhosa, 106

Jackson Makweta's Presidential Commission, 125
Jando, 8
job advertisements, 91–92

Kenya, community secondary schools in, 23
Kiswahili
    curriculum for schools, 12n26
    evolution of, 11–12
    as a language of instruction, 11–12, 14–17, 18, 24n56
    meaning of, 11n21
    as a medium of communication, 12
    as national language, 14n30
    as the official language of communication, 12–14
    Tanzanian researchers and, 3
    vs English, divisive tendencies and attitudes, 27–29
Kiswahili Journal, 13
"*Kiswanglish*", 48
knowledge gap among students, 52

language of instruction, in Tanzania, 29n71, 32n2. *See also* English; Kishwahili
languages of colonizers, 13n30
learning, defined by Ngaroga, 8. *See also* English
learning using other languages, 51–52

Madrasa, 8
mass media, role of, 130–31
Mbeya District Council, as an area of research, 68–72
    administration and land area, 69
    data collection from, 59–61
    educational information, 72
    industries, forests, and people's population, 71
    knowledge of English language and students' academic performance, 99–107
    performance in form four summative examinations, 82, 84
    responses from close-ended questionnaires, 84–99
    socio-economic and agricultural information, 70–71
    teachers' and students' general responses, 72–73
    transport and communication, 69–70
    water and energy supply, 70
memorized knowledge, using, 86, 88

Subject Index

Ministry of Education and Vocational Training (MoEVT), 29–30
mixed methods research design, defined, 58–59
mother tongue, defined, 11n19
motivation, among teachers' and students', 112, 119
Musoma Resolution (1974), 10

NACTE
    certificate level education, 18
    diploma education, 18
Namibian schools, English language in, 44
The National Higher Education Policy (1995), 10
national language, 14n30. *See also* Kishwahili
NECTA
    advanced secondary education under, 18
    ordinary secondary education, 18
    pre-primary education, 18
    primary education, 18
    Teacher Education Grade IIIa, 18
    teacher education under, 18
negative attitude towards English, 111. *See also* English

observation and experimental studies, 61
official language, 14n30. *See also* English; Kishwahili
Official System of Education, 16
Oman, use of English language in, 37–38
oral English learning, 41–42
ordinary secondary education, 18

parents
    role of, 131–32
    sensitization by mass media, 131
political science *(Siasa)* subjects, 16, 17, 21
population, defined, 62
postgraduate studies, 18
preparedness, for examinations, 115

pre-primary education, 18
primary education, 18
Presidential Commission for Education of 1980, 17
primary data, defined, 60–61
private secondary schools, 6, 18
private sectors in education, role of, 133–34
problem-posing education, 65n26

quality education, 23n55, 122–23
questionnaires, 61
Qur'an, 8

random sampling techniques, 62–63
research data, defined, 60
research design, defined, 56
research information, defined, 60
"Rights in Education and Self-Identity: Education and Language of Instruction in Namibia," 44
rural areas, poor performance in, 5–6

sampling design, defined, 62
sampling techniques, 62
Saudi Arabia, English language in, 40
school fees, abolition of, 10
secondary data, defined, 61
secondary education systems
    community secondary schools. *See* community secondary schools
    English as the language of instruction in, 13, 16, 19–20, 45, 113
    failure of students in, 84, 125–26
    Kiswahili as a medium of instruction, 117
    levels of, 19
    qualified teachers in, 130
"*Shule za Kata*," 23
Siasa (political science) subjects, 16, 17, 21
Socialism and Rural Development (1968), 10
South African Schools, English language in, 43–45

Subject Index

speaking English, inability in, 50, 107–13, 108
Special Package for Social Sciences (SPSS) programme, 84
Statistical Package for Social Sciences (SPSS), 64
students
    facilitator, 48
    poor performance in form four examinations, 113–15
"Students' Perceived Level of English Proficiency in Secondary Schools in Dodoma, Tanzania," 50

Tanganyika, 9, 10
Tanzania Commission for Universities (TCU) regulations, 128
Tanzanian educational policy, 122
Tanzanian educational system, 18–20
Tanzania Zambia Railways Authority (TAZARA) rail, 69–70
teachers. *See also* English language in Tanzania
    availability, 89–91
    competency, 43–44
    fluency in English language, 96–99
    lack of English proficiency among, 39–42
    need of effective training for, 43
    role of, 133
    in rural areas, 5
    teaching experiences, 91–92

Teacher Education Grade IIIa, 18
Teachers Grade, 22n51
teaching profession, criteria for taking up, 126–28, 130
teaching using other languages, 51–52
tertiary education, 13–14, 15, 18–20, 26, 45. *See also* secondary education systems
The Education Ordinance (1969), 10
"The Language of Instruction Issue in Tanzania," 10
trans-lingualism, 48
tribal language, 6
tutorial assistants (TAs), 128

Ujamaa, 9, 12
unemployment rate among youths, 71
Universal Primary Education (UPE), 10, 22, 22n51
University of Dar es Salaam, 15, 16
university level education, 18
Unyago, 8

vernacular languages of Tanzanian ethnic groups, 45n26, 109, 111, 124
VETA, vocational education under, 18
Vietnam, English language in, 36, 46–47
Villagization (1973), 10
vocational education under VETA, 18

writing skills, 107

www.ingramcontent.com/pod-product-compliance
Lightning Source LLC
Chambersburg PA
CBHW062002180426
43198CB00036B/2143